Young Man,

BE STRONG

Young Man,

BE STRONG

David G. Burkholder

Rod and Staff Publishers, Inc.
P.O. Box 3, Hwy. 172
Crockett, Kentucky 41413
Telephone: (606) 522-4348

Cover photos: Robert Eby

Copyright 1988
By David G. Burkholder

Printed in U.S.A.

Hardcover Edition   ISBN 0-7399-2414-1
Catalog no. 2485

Paper Edition   ISBN 0-7399-2415-X
Catalog no. 2486

13   14   15   16   17   —   18   17   16   15   14   13   12   11   10   09

Dedication

To young men everywhere who desire to be strong for God, and to our own sons in particular.

CONTENTS

Foreword

This book is a most welcome addition to the literature intended to guide young men toward the nobler purposes of life and prepare them for a rewarding eternity. Even though other volumes have been written addressing our boys, there is something distinctive about this book.

The author grew up in a conservative Mennonite home in southeastern Pennsylvania. In 1978, he with his family responded to the call of the Mission Board of the Eastern Pennsylvania Mennonite Church and Related Areas to serve in Burns Lake, British Columbia, Canada. He is presently raising his own family and serving in the ministry in that area.

The book calls for a self-abandoning commitment to Jesus Christ, which results in a sane and sober outlook on life. The style of writing, however, captivates the reader's interest. The author presents a philosophy of life that has been born, not only behind a desk, but out of practical experiences and observations.

The book does not constitute an in-depth study of the Scriptures on the subjects considered. Sound Scriptural concepts are substantiated with some Scripture references. A unique contribution of this treatise is the broad scope of its coverage. A careful reading and study of its contents will certainly result in a proper and comprehensive outlook for life. The principles which are applied can help the serious young man to find his way through what the book does not deal with directly.

This book is written with the developing teenager in mind. It should help young men to establish proper ideals for life and thereby escape the many pitfalls that confront the youth of our day. It will also prove to be most helpful to instruct parents who sense a need for reference materials on this subject.

May God help both young and old to lay hold of His provisions, to guide our youth to the shores of safety in this end time.

—Isaac K. Sensenig

Introduction

Young men have tremendous potential—for good or for bad. God and Satan both know this. Both are keenly competing for young men's loyalty and lives. The winner takes all. Satan brings his victims down to eternal ruin, while God brings those who follow Him to real life and eternal blessing.

This book was written to help young men see the real issues of life from a practical viewpoint. The earlier chapters show what a young man needs to be, and the later ones are intended to show how to apply Bible principles to daily life.

No book could speak of every decision and problem a young man will face. This book tries to say enough to help equip a young man to face that which is yet unknown.

If God can use this book to touch and draw young men to Himself, its purpose is accomplished. May every reader be inspired to set his sights on a noble life here and now, and on a blessed eternity with God.

Acknowledgments

First of all, to God for giving me the privilege to be His son. Any usefulness encouraged by this book is to His praise and glory.

To those who have guided and influenced my life in the past, and to those who encouraged me in the writing of this book.

To the numerous brethren who have offered valuable advice and have given their time reviewing the manuscripts. Special appreciation to David L. Martin for his editorial assistance.

To my family for their support, sacrifice, and patience while the book was being written.

Chapter 1

It's Your Day

Young man, today is your day! Childhood is behind you, and you must become a man. Today is the time to be sure you are moving toward manhood in the right way. Now is the time to determine that you will make your day count—not only for yourself, but for God. Now is the time to look ahead and think about where you are going.

You as a young man stand in an awesome position. Your potential for success or failure is staggering. In the next few years, you will make decisions that have the potential to make you or break you. The effect of those decisions will follow you the rest of your life. You can't afford to take the next few years lightly.

Look around you. See what other young men have done with their day. No doubt many grown men wish they could go back ten years to your age and start over. But they can't. Neither will you be able to go back ten years from now and start over. What you do with your day, right now, is very important.

Look back. Think about some young men who succeeded in their day. It will encourage you to see that young men can overcome and be faithful. Make young men like Joseph and Daniel examples you want to follow. God needs young men like that today. He wants you to be one of them.

Not long ago (it seems at least), I stood where you stand. It was my day. Pressures and decisions were forced upon me. Looking back now, I realize more and more how crucial those years of young manhood were. How the effect of those decisions follows me—even today! I must confess that many times I didn't understand how far-reaching they were and where they would lead me. I shudder when I think, "What if . . . ?"

But God was merciful and gracious to me. That is the only reason I have anything worthwhile to share. God put many influences in my pathway to help me go right. My home, the church, and many other people encouraged me. Sometimes He used circumstances or even a book to help me. I thank Him for them all.

That is why I am writing to you now. Others have helped me, and now I want to encourage you in whatever way I can. The story is told of an old man who crossed a deep ravine, obviously for the last time. Instead of going on, he stopped and built a bridge across the ravine. When asked why he went to all that effort, he replied that he wanted to make it easier for the young man coming after him. I hope the Lord can use this book to put in some bridges for you.

My purpose is not to talk to you so much as an instructor, but as a father. It is my desire to have you travel with me through this book. Let's share the struggles, the battles, and the victories together. Surely, as we seek God's will together, it can be of benefit to you.

Here is a poem whose author I do not know. But his thought fits well here.

At the Crossroads

He stood at the crossroads all alone,
The sunrise in his face;
He had no thought for the world unknown—
He was set for a manly race.

But the road stretched east and the road stretched west,
And the boy did not know which road was best,
So he took the wrong road and went down,
And he lost the race and the victor's crown.

He was caught at last in an angry snare
Because none stood at the crossroads there
To show him the better road.

Another day at the selfsame place,
A boy with high hopes stood;
He too was set for a manly race,
He was seeking the things that were good.

But one was there who the roads did know,
And that one showed him which way to go.
So he turned away from the road that went down,
And he won the race and the victor's crown.

He walks today the highways fair
Because one stood at the crossroads there,
To show him the better way.

Now I'm not claiming to know everything you will need to know. But I do know there are basic Bible principles that will help you face anything, no matter how new or unusual. And, as in any other problem in life, you can use what you do know to face the unknown. That is what this book is about—laying down principles that will help you find answers to problems and tests none of us even know about yet.

You know the devil is trying to spoil your day. He is out there trying to ruin every young man that comes along. How successful he has been with far too many other men! He will be busy laying all kinds of traps for you too.

But you do not need to be caught, because you do not need to walk alone. God wants to help you face your day. Then, instead of stepping into Satan's traps, you will take steppingstone after steppingstone to glory. God will be as pleased about that as you will be.

Of course, God will not do it all for you. There are things you yourself must do. You can't just drift along, because there is a strong current going the wrong way. You must be strong and overcome that current, or else you will be as helpless as a boat without a motor above the Niagara Falls— swept to destruction. If you do not do your part, God cannot help you as He wants to.

But don't sigh about needing to do your part. Rather, look at your day as a day of opportunity. Make it count for you and God. Then God will do for you what you cannot do for yourself.

So let's travel together. Most important, let's travel together with God. Then your day is bound to be good—now and eternally.

Chapter 2

When It's Your Turn

Perhaps you have never thought about it, but just now you may be experiencing the most carefree years you will ever have. Likely you have no family to support, your health is probably good, and you are nearly as strong as you will ever be. Because so many things may be going your way, you can easily begin to think that living in the present is what life is all about. But you must look beyond the present and remember that what you do now will affect the future.

Young men can become too intense and impatient about the things of time. Certain goals can become more important to them than they should. They can be like Esau. When Jacob offered to trade his food for Esau's birthright, Esau said he may as well because if he didn't eat right now, he would die from starvation. Had he looked ahead, he would probably have done differently.

My father used to tell us boys to think ahead five years and see if we still thought that what we wanted was a good idea. Ten years would probably be better yet. Actually, looking on into eternity is what my father really meant.

A story is told about a splendid band of musicians. Every

member seemed to do his part. Their individual parts blended in perfect harmony.

Things were going well for the players until one day it was announced that every member had to play a solo. One trumpeter was horrified. When his turn finally came, he raised his trumpet. But not a sound came out. Everyone waited, but there was only silence—a deathly silence. His fellow players were stunned. The truth was that he could not play!

For two years he had been part of the band. Outwardly, he had performed splendidly. He had raised his trumpet and blown up his cheeks just like all the others. But the moment of truth had come. He could not play. He never had played. He had had all the motions, but no music. He had been a first-class hypocrite.

We might ask, "Didn't he know there was a day coming when the truth would come out? Wouldn't it have been better if he had never joined?"

The answer to his problem seems easy, doesn't it? But he is so typical of how many people live. They go through all the motions of life. They go to church just as if they loved the Lord. They obey the law, talk pleasantly, try to live a decent moral life, and maybe even pray and read the Bible, as they have seen godly people do. But they ignore the fact that sometime they must do their solo before Almighty God. God will expose their inner emptiness just as the musician was exposed. He knows if people are living by true heart love for Him, or if they are just going through hollow motions.

Young man, someday you too must stand before God and give an account of yourself. You will have to play your own solo. Not only your actions but also your motives will be exposed. The full truth will come out. It's sobering, isn't it?

And it should be. The outcome will be for all eternity.

That doesn't mean that you need to end up like the musician—dreadfully embarrassed. If you think ahead to the time when it will be your turn, and live genuinely, you have nothing to fear. God wants you to take sober warning, but then to go on and live a happy, satisfying life.

God said it like this: "Rejoice, O young man, in thy youth; and let thy heart cheer thee in the days of thy youth, and walk in the ways of thine heart, and in the sight of thine eyes: but know thou, that for all these things God will bring thee into judgment" (Ecclesiastes 11:9).

Some young men like that verse until they come to the last part that tells of accountability. They think that part spoils all the rejoicing they hope to have. Do you think it does? Did God get it all mixed up? Is He suggesting that you "live it up" and then pay for it at the Judgment?

Of course not! I repeat, God wants you to have a happy, satisfying life. He is not a spoilsport, as some people think. God looks at more than just the present. He knows what will finally be best for you—not only in life, but in eternity.

God really wants you to pay attention to the whole verse. If you realize that you must give account, and allow that fact to help you to do right, you can indeed enjoy the days of youth. I expect that you have already discovered that you are happiest when you do what you know you ought to do.

Young men sometimes act as if living for the flesh is really great. But, as the saying goes, "It isn't what it's cracked up to be." The fun only lasts for a short time. When the pleasure disappears, the dues are extremely high. Someone described this disappointment as "the high cost of low living." Don't be fooled by the glitter and glamour of sin and self-seeking.

Young Man, Be Strong

Recently someone did a survey of a number of the popular stars in the entertainment world. Their record of broken homes, misery, drugs, and suicide certainly shows that the present, even at its "best," does not satisfy. The personal lives of some of the most envied and glamorized people prove it again and again. God settles some accounts sooner, some later; but sooner or later the accounting day comes.

Accountability—none of us can ever escape it. Actually, why should we want to? Look at the people who live as if there is none. See all the difficulty and debauchery they get themselves into. Accepting accountability—that's where safety lies. When you are tempted or you must make a decision, just remember that someday (and you don't know how soon) you must answer for what you do. It will give you strength to live a life you will never need to be ashamed of.

Chapter 3

Set Your Goals

How would you like riding in a car that has no steering wheel or sailing in a ship that has no rudder? Goals are to us what a steering wheel is to a car and a rudder is to a ship. For another way of saying it, goals make the difference between a pilgrim and a tramp. Goals help our journey of life to make sense.

Perhaps you have noticed that, in the world of money, some people seem to stumble onto success. They always seem to be at the right place at the right time. Everything they touch seems to turn to gold. At least that is how it looks to us. Is it really that way? Ask them. They would be quick to tell you it isn't that way at all. Rather, they would insist that their progress is the result of setting goals and then setting out to reach them. Everything they do is geared to reach that goal. It becomes the passion of their lives.

A young girl in our community was a member of the Canadian Olympic Cross-Country Skiing Team. She practiced winter and summer. In the winter, it was in the snow. In the summer, she put wheels on her skis and practiced on the shoulder of the highway. Finally she went off to a training camp to practice with her teammates. Her father said she had not been able to spend as much time as she wanted in her training at home. She wanted to put all her energies toward her goal.

The coach of a very successful basketball team demanded that his players "eat and sleep" basketball. He knew what it takes to play well.

People do all that just to reach an earthly goal. Of course you know that the Christian has far greater goals than that. But the way some people sacrifice for an earthly goal shows us how much we need to put into gaining our heavenly goal.

Let's try to analyze

Why You Need Goals

There are all kinds of earthly opportunities in the world. You could use all your energies making money. Or you could go after prestige in business or politics. You could spend your life just enjoying yourself in pleasure and sports. You know too that this is about as far as many people think when they set their goals.

Knowing what other people live for puts pressure on you. It would be easy to let other people's passion for making money get hold of you, because you have the responsibility to earn a living too. You must have higher goals than that, or you will become earthy and forget about the ultimate goal. When you dig a ditch, you dig it as straight to your goal as you can—unless you like digging ditches better than most of us do. In the same way, you want to work straight toward your most important goal in life and not get stuck in the earth of this world.

Goals protect you. When you keep clear sight of where you want to go, earthly pursuits will not have nearly so much grip on you. You will be able to detect it more quickly when you drift off course. For example, when Nehemiah was busy overseeing the wall-building at Jerusalem, some enemies came and offered to help build. Although Nehemiah was eager to get done quickly, he knew that his goal was not just to have a wall, but to have a good wall. So he refused their offer.

Then his enemies tried another trick to stop the work. They invited him to a meeting. Nehemiah would not go. He said, "I am doing a great work, so that I cannot come down: why should the work cease, whilst I leave it, and come down to you?" His goal protected him from these tricks.

Goals give you purpose. Not having anything worth doing destroys your incentive to get up and going in the morning. Purpose generates energy. Because goals put you to work, you make progress, and this causes a good feeling. This principle works in the spiritual part of life as well.

Before we discuss how to set goals, there is a simple question that can help you get started right. That is,

Who Sets Your Goals?

Doesn't each of us set his own goals? Yes and no. How do we decide which goals to set? Often it's by letting other people influence our decisions. When you must make a decision, do you look to see what some worldly neighbor of yours is doing? If you do, the world is setting your goals.

Even if worldly influence doesn't quite convince you to set worldly goals, it can still make your goals fuzzy. We tend to want what has been called the best of both worlds. We can be like the boy who was asked which of the two men in Luke 16 he would rather be like: the rich man or Lazarus. He said he would like to live like the rich man and die like Lazarus! That's the problem of conflicting goals—they will never work. That boy really wasn't too much different from the people in Jesus' day who "loved the praise of men more than the praise of God." It isn't hard to know where they ended up.

Young man, if you are serious about life, you will want your goals to please the right people, and God. Are you ready to let God be the chief influence in setting your goals? If so, we can go on to discuss

How to Set Goals

Setting grand goals is easy. But these goals can be like many people's New Year's resolutions. Those kind are not worth much. Setting a serious goal is more than a once-and-done matter. It means making a series of right choices.

Choices produce a course. One choice leads to another. Some are more pivotal than others. Some seem small and insignificant but are part of an irreversible course. Not far from where we live is a triple continental divide. From this spot the water flows in three different directions. It flows east to the Atlantic Ocean, west to the Pacific, and north to the Arctic Ocean. At this mountaintop spot, a rock in the mud or a tuft of grass could easily divert water from one ocean to another. A breeze in the rain could put droplets on one side or the other. Drops at the top may be so close together but yet at the bottom be forever separated, thousands of miles apart.

Many choices are like that. They seem ever so insignificant. But they help to determine a destiny. They are like a mountain stream that trickles away from its source, and then tumbles and finally rushes along, all the while becoming more powerful—sweeping toward a goal.

You are standing at the mountaintop of your life. The

choices you as a young man make have the same effect on your life. That is why it is very important that you start the stream off right.

Choices work both ways—for good and for bad. The songwriter wrote, "Each vict'ry will help you some other to win." On the other hand, take Samson. He chose to flirt boldly with sin. He dared to go back to Delilah again and again even though she tried to betray him. Every time he escaped the trap and fled in triumph. That is, every time but once— the last time. One choice, two choices, three choices—deeper and deeper until he was caught.

You are making serious choices every day. Satan will try to get you to think your choices do not matter, because you are young. But that is not true. Many a young man out there made choices at your age that make it hard for him now to come back to the narrow road. It might be the woman he married or the career he chose. But it might also be smaller choices—the friends he spent time with, the magazines he read, or how he spent his free afternoons.

Now, what goals should a young man set? It is not so important whether you choose to be a carpenter or a mechanic, but rather how you will fare spiritually. The occupation, the car, or the house you choose will come and go. But your soul will endure.

Five Goals to Live For

The goals that follow might seem obvious to you. You might say you have had these goals for a long time without ever putting them into words. Fine, but the fact is that some young men don't have them. They are thinking about getting a car, getting a girlfriend, and being accepted with their friends, and that's about as far as they think. So don't skim these goals too rapidly!

1. *First, you need the goal to please God and finally to be with Him in glory.* That goal must influence any other goals you have. If your goal is to visit New York City but you spend your time touring the Grand Canyon, will you make it to New York by the skin of your teeth? No, you won't get there at all. Neither is there any such thing as living only for earthly goals and then getting to heaven by the skin of your teeth.

2. *Another goal you should have is to find real purpose and fulfillment in life.* Life does not have to be easy if it is worthwhile. Even ungodly people know this, as you can see by how they work and sweat to build muscles or make money. But they will never find fulfillment where they are seeking it. Fulfillment comes by living under God's blessing and approval.

3. *You should also be concerned that you are worthy of your profession as a child of God.* Recently, I met a doctor who worked with all the doctors in his state who were addicted to drugs. If they failed to respond to treatment, he had to strip them of their license to practice medicine, because they were not worthy of their profession. Your goal must be to not bring any shame on your Lord.

4. *Another goal to set clearly before yourself is to be active in service to God.* The Christian's life is not his own. He has been bought with blood. In return, he shows his love to God by serving Him—not just out of duty but in loyal devotion. Plan to do it with all your heart.

5. *The last goal covers a wide range. It is the goal of being an asset to society.* This means wanting to leave the world a better place for your being here. You should prefer giving over receiving. Your employer ought to benefit because you

work for him. Your home should miss your input when you are gone. President Eisenhower puzzled some people when he bought a run-down farm. He explained that he liked having a farm he could improve. You need to think like this about all of life.

Perhaps you were looking for advice on more practical goals, like handling money properly or knowing what kind of job fits your abilities. We'll look at those matters in later chapters. In the meantime, remember to be realistic about those practical goals. Don't make job or payment commitments that interfere with your spiritual goals. Remember that the greatest goals in life are for the welfare of your soul.

Keep in mind also that if you always think of the most important goals first, they can help you find your way in setting the smaller, practical goals. Now let me share a few principles that suggest

How to Reach Your Goals

Reaching any worthwhile goal requires purpose. God is a good demonstrator of that. As soon as Adam and Eve sinned, God promised a Redeemer. For centuries He moved toward the right time to bring Jesus into the world. He never lost sight of that goal, and finally He brought it to pass. Now He has goals for us. Best of all, He wants to help us reach them.

Another outstanding example of goal reaching is Daniel. How could he do it? The Bible tells us he "purposed in his heart." And what he purposed, he did. God honored his noble purpose and helped him.

Look at any successful believer and you will see that sense of purpose. Successful Christians are ready to work and suffer to succeed. There are no quitters among them.

Young Man, Be Strong

When Ruth of old left her heathen nation, she did it with purpose. Listen to her ringing determination: "Intreat me not to leave thee, or to return from following after thee: for whither thou goest, I will go; and where thou lodgest, I will lodge: thy people shall be my people, and thy God my God: where thou diest, will I die, and there will I be buried." She succeeded, while Orpah, her sister-in-law, turned back and was never heard of among God's people again.

Closely tied to purpose is perseverance. Some people start well but never finish. A neighbor of ours was building a hay barn. He even got as far as having the rafters placed. But today only the concrete pads are left because he never finished. That is merely sad, but when people do that with their lives, it is tragic.

It also takes planning to reach your goals. Plan your life the way you would plan a long trip. After all, life is the greatest journey you will ever take. Not long ago, I came across a list of purposes that one man purposed to make the guide for his life. Maybe you should make a list of your goals as you read on in this book. Then you can use them to check on yourself as you go through life.

Purpose, plan, and persevere. Young man, put these into practice, and God will reveal goals He has for you that as yet you know nothing about.

Chapter 4

Know Your Enemy

An artist once painted a picture of a chess game between Satan and a young man. The chessboard was set in such a way that there appeared to be no way for the young man to escape. The young man's horror was distressing to see. Finally a master player was called to see if there were any way the young man could win. He studied the picture for a long time. Suddenly he shouted, "Young man, make *that* move. That's the move!" There was a way out after all!

Young man, you are not in a chess game. You are in something far more important than that. You are in a life-and-death battle with Satan! He is constantly scheming to catch you off guard. And if you are not alert, he will win. Let me tell you though that you don't need to be one of the losers. By facing him God's way and by God's help, you can be strong and overcome Satan.

But it won't be easy. You can expect a lifelong battle with him. Now, at the start of your life, you need to prepare yourself well for the conflict.

First, you need to realize

What Your Enemy Is Like

Satan is a real person—not a human, of course, but a person, just as God and the angels are. He can think. He can love—or at least he could at one time—and he can hate. Maybe you thought no one hates you, but Satan does.

Now we don't want to become too preoccupied thinking about our personal enemy. But we certainly don't want to let him become too hazy in our thinking. It is said of Luther that he once felt Satan's presence in the room with him so strongly that he threw an ink bottle at him. Of course he missed, but he had a literal impression of how real Satan is.

Surprisingly, it appears that Satan had a good start! The Bible indicates in Isaiah 14, Ezekiel 28, and elsewhere that he was one of the chief angels. But he was not satisfied; he wanted to be like God. The result? Jesus said, "I beheld Satan as lightning fall from heaven."

What future was left for Satan? The beauty, the dignity, and the light were gone forever, and all he could look forward to was horrors of darkness and torture. He was forever doomed. But God allowed him access to the earth. Satan set his heart on venting his spite on God while he still had the chance. Now he is trying to spoil God's purposes wherever he can. His specialty is wrecking people, the crown of God's creation. You and I are both among his targets.

The Bible tells us that Satan often comes to people as an angel of light. In other words, he is a master deceiver. If people saw him as he is and saw where his suggestions would take them, would they listen? Never. So he uses salesmanship.

The interesting thing is that he often injects and mixes the truth into his temptations. He told Eve, "God doth know that in the day ye eat thereof, then your eyes shall be opened, and ye shall be as gods, knowing good and evil." Every word of that was true, right? But Satan was implying a big lie, which was, "God is keeping something from you that you have the right to enjoy."

After it was all over, it is not hard to guess that Eve mourned, "He told me I would know good and evil, and that was true. But I already knew all the good I wanted, so all I learned was evil!"

An acquaintance of mine says, "When I got converted, the devil told me I would lose my friends, and that was one time the devil didn't lie. I did lose them." But the devil deliberately failed to mention that after he was converted, he would have new friends better than the ones he lost.

Satan comes as an angel of light to revival meetings. And he says to many a young man, in effect, "Don't get too excited. You're already a church member. If you think something is wrong with your spiritual life, go home and pray about it. But don't make a public commitment." He will even say this to someone who has neither prayed nor said a word of love for the Lord for half a year.

Beside that man sits another young man who is right with God but is struggling. He had made an unkind comment this morning. Should he make a public confession? Then he hears the preacher read a reassuring verse and realizes he can confess some things personally to God and to the person he offended. Just as he grasps this ray of light, along comes one of Satan's demons and tries to take away any feeling of true assurance. As you can expect, Satan always tries to get us to feel the opposite from the way it really is.

Of course, hardly anyone really hears Satan whisper. But he has a way of injecting thoughts and making them seem as if they came out of one's own mind.

Satan is religious. Is that a new thought to you? He knows that humans are incurably religious, so he offers a sidetrack religion. The saying goes, "Where God builds a church, the devil builds a chapel hard by." He actually promotes some forms of godliness. But the types he promotes are religions that ignore repentance, the need of a personal Saviour, and a life of obedience to Jesus Christ. He likes people to carry a Bible around as long as they do not accept it as the final authority. The apostle Paul described these people as those who have "a form of godliness, but [deny] the power thereof."

Even true Christians need to watch out lest Satan sidetracks them. If you like to read, beware! It's surprising how many Christians who would never read a book written by a Jehovah's Witness will drink in literature written by other men who are not sound in the faith, as if it were pure water. Look what Satan is offering in today's publications. Instead of God's radical change of conversion, he offers mere self-improvement—ways to improve your self-image or your lifestyle. Satan's real purpose is to turn heads away from the Answer to less important things.

The same is true for positive thinking. Thinking positively is fine. Having faith is fine. But it becomes a trap when we begin to forget that God is the one who controls our lives, not our faith and positive thinking!

Satan does not mind exposing himself after he has used his victims. He is just like a lion that sneaks up silently, kills his prey, and then devours openly. The social drinker and the drug experimenter finally admit that they are addicted after they have lost their money and disgraced themselves. A young man who starts listening to the false, partial-gospel radio preachers can wind up spiritually far, far from home. Then it is obvious who his master was all the time. But by that time, such people often show surprisingly little interest in the Lord's deliverance. Besides, Satan makes them think deliverance is hopeless.

Mark it down that you are no match for this enemy of yours. No person on earth can hope to overcome him alone. He has an endless list of traps he uses. We'll touch a few in thinking about

How He Tries to Trap You

Long ago the Greeks tried to capture the city of Troy. They besieged the city for a long time but couldn't take it. Before they sailed away, they built a large wooden horse and left it behind. Triumphantly, the citizens of Troy took the horse inside the city as a trophy of their success. What they didn't know was that inside that horse were Greek soldiers. That night the Greek soldiers slipped out of the horse and opened the city gates for the Greek army, which had returned and was waiting outside. The people of Troy had resisted the outer invasion. But they were taken from within.

This demonstrates how Satan works. He is no less clever than the Greeks were. And how does he try to take you from within?

He tries to get you used to sin. Profanity that once shocked you when you heard it might not seem so bad anymore. Immorality among your neighbors or relatives might seem hardly worth a shrug. People smirk today over how easily shocked people were back in the 1950s. The fact is, people of the '50s were wiser than the people of today. The apostle Paul, writing to the Corinthians, said, "It is reported commonly that there is fornication among you, and such fornication as is not so much as named among the Gentiles. . . . And ye are puffed up, and have not rather mourned, that he that hath done this deed might be taken away from among you." It seems the Corinthians felt smug about how much sin they could put up with without being shocked. Paul in effect told them, "It's out of style to be shocked these days, but there are times when you *ought* to be shocked!"

Sin is like danger. People who live with it every day forget how dangerous it is. In our local logging industry, being a tree feller is one of the most dangerous jobs. Many things can happen to a person who cuts trees down day after day. Trees can fall the wrong way, tops may break off, or trees leaning against each other can take the feller by surprise. But strangely, often it is not the beginners who are injured. Rather, it is those who have been at it a long time. Why? They become too familiar with danger and do not respect the threats. They start taking chances.

Satan wants you to underestimate him. Boaters have learned about underestimation the hard way on the Niagara River. The closer one comes to the falls, the stronger the current becomes. Taking chances, boaters have suddenly found themselves drawn toward the falls. If their boat motor was not powerful enough or failed, they were swept over.

Some people become downright reckless about sin. They seem to enjoy playing around with sin and thinking they are getting by with it. There is something alluring about the challenge that draws people into it.

People who dare sin are like those who dared Niagara Falls. They would go down over the falls in barrels and various other contraptions—just to see if they could make it alive. The museum in the city there has the beat-up remains of the barrels. It tells you which ones made it and which ones did not.

One man even dared to try to row a boat across the river

just above the falls. Finally he lost the struggle and was swept toward the edge. He managed to grab a rock and hang onto it for a while. But before rescue came, he lost his grip and vanished over the falls.

Many a young man slips because he takes the kind of attitude that man had. He is a Christian, and he feels he can handle the evil atmosphere where he works. But slowly he begins to slip. Before he realizes it, he is laughing at things he never thought he would laugh at and telling jokes he never thought he would tell. He had felt capable of handling a dangerous situation. Then the temptation came on like the current above Niagara Falls, and by the time he realized what was happening, he didn't know how to catch himself.

Confidence is wonderful. But never feel confident enough to take risks with temptation.

You may think that we older ones make too much of the danger of sin. You may feel we don't trust you. In a sense, that's true; we don't trust ourselves either! Our fears for you come from our own battles with Satan. We know how quickly we can sin if we toy with sin. We want to spare you some of the failures we have had.

Satan wants you to nurse your carnal nature. A Christian's new nature is dead to the things he once thought he must enjoy. Now he enjoys obeying God. But his old nature is not so dead that he can't feed it. If he gives just a few minutes of pampering to his old nature, it will roar to life again. "Every man is tempted, when he is drawn away of his own lust, and enticed." Satan knows this. That old nature likes to open your heart's door to him. Keep it dead!

To overcome Satan, you must have ways of

Dealing With Your Enemy

Greek mythology tells of an island from which came the most beautiful and alluring music. However, anyone who sailed near it disappeared. Many sailors lost their lives there. The island was famous for its treachery.

The story tells of some who succeeded in resisting the temptation. One captain is said to have filled his sailors' ears with wax and had himself tied to the masthead when they sailed by the island. Shutting it all out was his method.

Another captain solved the problem of allurement by seeing to it that his own ship had better music on board than that which came from the island. He and his satisfied crew sailed safely by the island because they were content with what they had.

It will take a combination of the two captains' methods for you to sail safely by all that your enemy will put into your way. You will have to stop your ears to his temptations. Even more often, you will have to stop your eyes. You will need to be stern with yourself. As Jesus said, "If thy right eye offend thee, pluck it out." You will need to say no and mean no.

Also, you need to know that the joy you have in living right is better than the pleasure Satan offers. Many people can assure you that God's joy *is* better. And they are developing more and more of a taste for it!

Besides these two methods, here are several other suggestions.

Remember what a liar Satan is. Don't let him make you believe that any religion is good enough and whatever you call right is right. Don't be caught by thinking the easy way leads to heaven, when Jesus said the way to heaven is narrow. Be wary of those who talk right but don't live right.

Their way is empty and headed for disaster.

You must be determined. You must hate sin personally. Personal determination by itself is not nearly enough, but you can't do without it.

Above all else, *lean hard on God.* Near the beginning, you read that we should not be too preoccupied with Satan. That would be unhealthy. To be successful over Satan, we must look to God, our deliverer! He is a personal friend as real as our personal enemy. "Greater is he that is in you, than he that is in the world."

Chapter 5

What Everybody Needs

Everybody has needs. Some needs are more important than others. What everybody needs the most is a right relationship with God. But everyone is born with a sinful nature. This automatically puts us into a wrong relationship with God. To enter heaven and be with God, we must somehow be delivered from the power of this sinful nature.

Nothing less than full deliverance will do. Some young men (and others too) try to feed the lusts of their sinful nature and still call themselves Christians. This never works and only results in frustration and misery—and finally in disaster.

The good news is that we do not need to stay a slave to our sinful nature (what the Bible also calls the flesh, the carnal nature, or the old man). Neither do we need to settle for half deliverance, which is no deliverance at all. God has a way to change us into what He wants. First you need to recognize

What You Are by Nature

A preacher supposedly announced a funeral to his congregation. The day arrived, and the audience gathered. The pastor preached a stirring sermon that made the tears flow. To the congregation's surprise, he had nothing good to say about the deceased. Instead, he thoroughly condemned the one in the casket. The pastor told how sly and deceitful he had been. The congregation was appalled. How mean!

Finally the casket was opened, and the congregation filed past to see the remains of this person they had heard so much about. To their shock, what was in the casket but a mirror! They saw only themselves! The pastor was trying to teach the members how evil their carnal nature is.

Jesus said, "For from within, out of the heart of men, proceed evil thoughts, adulteries, fornications, murders, thefts, covetousness, wickedness, deceit, lasciviousness, an evil eye, blasphemy, pride, foolishness: all these evil things come from within, and defile the man." He was saying that about all men—including you and me.

The prophet Jeremiah put it like this: "The heart is deceitful above all things, and desperately wicked: who can know it?"

The apostle Paul adds to this picture by saying, "Wherein in time past ye walked according to the course of this world, according to the prince of the power of the air, the spirit that now worketh in the children of disobedience: among whom also we all had our conversation in times past in the lusts of our flesh, fulfilling the desires of the flesh and of the mind; and were by nature the children of wrath, even as others."

These Scriptures show us what we are like by nature. We are bad from birth. No one needed to teach us to do wrong. Ever since Adam and Eve chose to disobey God and serve the flesh, the whole human race has been in the clutches of its own sinful nature. The grip is so strong that man is powerless to break this bondage by himself.

You no doubt have become aware of this force in your own life. The tendency to lie and deceive is in everyone. After some wrongdoing, you have probably thought in despair, "How could I have done that?" Then you may have been equally surprised at yourself to discover your tendency to cover up the wrong through some kind of deceitfulness. It may be hard to understand how you could have yielded to the temptations. But really, it is just what the carnal nature leads one to do.

The nature of man is to serve himself. He wants what he wants regardless of whether it is right or not. Of course, the devil capitalizes on this tendency and inflames temptation and lust in every way he can.

You need not be surprised at the temptations to pride, selfishness, stubbornness, or resistance to instruction and authority. Note that I said "temptations." Most people have enough restraint not to be totally mastered by their temptations. By training and practice, people can quit using foul language, cut down smoking, polish up their lives. But no one ever becomes good enough to be delivered from himself and so be acceptable to God.

The apostle Paul explains in Romans 7:18, 19 how it works: "For I know that in me (that is, in my flesh,) dwelleth no good thing: for to will is present with me; but how to perform that which is good I find not. For the good that I would I do not: but the evil which I would not, that I do." A person can want to and try to overcome his own evil tendencies, but he will never succeed satisfactorily. He can try everything, but will end by sinning all over again. That's the reason for the desperate cry of verse 24: "O wretched man that I am! who shall deliver me from the body of this death?" Thank God, there is an answer! "I thank God through Jesus

Christ our Lord" (verse 25).

No one needs to stay a slave to himself and sin. The good news of the Gospel is that God has a way for all to be set free. Let me explain

What God Can Make You

Sometimes you can overhaul an engine and make it like new. But if it's too bad, you have to start over with a new one. God could not fix us up and call us good enough. He had to give us a completely new start.

Jesus said, "Ye must be born again." This is the place God begins with us. None of our goodness or cleaning up impresses God. Neither do our excuses or self-justification. We are guilty before God on two counts: first, for being sinful by nature, which we just discussed; and second, for having committed sin.

So, we have two basic needs. We must be delivered from our own sinful nature, and we must be forgiven for the sins we have committed. God has made both of those possible. Sometimes we call His provision "the plan of salvation."

God is just. He could not simply overlook sin. It had to be accounted for. What would be the price of redeeming us? Could a guilty man simply die to pay for his sins and then go to heaven? No one could die to redeem himself. Justice demanded a sacrifice by someone who had never sinned. To redeem us would take the blood of a perfect person. Of course, there was no one on earth like that, so the Son of God, Jesus, became a man to live and die for the human race.

This was no simple matter. Jesus had to face all the temptations and trials of humanity and still remain perfect. He succeeded, and bled and died to ransom us from our sin. When He died He declared, "It is finished."

Now God could forgive sin. As 1 John 1:9 tells us, "He is faithful and just to forgive us our sins." As you meet the conditions God has laid down, God forgives you.

One term the Bible uses to describe the result of forgiveness of sin is *justification*. Justification is to be completely freed from all sin and be restored as if we had never done it. Think of it like this: Just as if I had never sinned. Romans 5:1 tells us, "Therefore being justified by faith, we have peace with God through our Lord Jesus Christ." Even though it is hard to fathom such restoration, the Bible tells us that God accepts those who come to Him like that. Isn't it wonderful?

Another inspiring fact is that God is not interested in merely cleansing us and then sending us out on our own again. We are spiritual orphans and would quickly lose our way. So what does God do? He adopts us as His children. How wonderful! Listen to it from Galatians 4:7: "Wherefore thou art no more a servant, but a son; and if a son, then an heir of God through Christ." Instead of being children of the wicked one, we are adopted into the family of God!

After giving a whole list of sins that will not enter heaven, He says in 1 Corinthians 6:11, "And such were some of you: but ye are washed, but ye are sanctified, but ye are justified in the name of the Lord Jesus, and by the Spirit of our God." Look where He found us—among the unrighteous—and then what He makes of us!

This verse also tells us how the cleansing takes place. The washing is by the blood of Jesus Christ. As you open your heart to God, the Holy Spirit enters to make your heart His home. He then takes charge and gives you the desire to be a faithful child and be worthy of the name.

All this is a radical change. The Bible calls it the new

birth. Can it be explained? Like seeing a sunset or feeling a breeze, you have to see and feel it to really know. Like the little old lady said, "It's better felt then telt." Now that is certainly true. But there is a lot more to it than mere feeling. There are some obvious results when a person experiences the new birth that prove it really happened.

The Bible says, "Therefore if any man be in Christ, he is a new creature: old things are passed away; behold, all things are become new." When that happens, you have a whole new outlook on life. Now you are free in conscience. The cloud of condemnation before God is gone. Instead, you feel love and acceptance because now you are in fellowship with God.

Now you hate the sin you once loved and love the right you once avoided. Why? Because now you love the things that your new Master, God, loves and hate what He hates.

Along with this comes a new desire to do right. The new nature wants to do right just like the old nature wanted to do wrong. God has done a special work of grace in your heart. "For it is God which worketh in you both to will and to do of his good pleasure" (Philippians 2:13). The desire to please God is one of the most prominent evidences of the work of God in the heart. This then is naturally followed by a sincere effort "to do of his good pleasure."

Now you want to please God. And why not? If you owed a million dollars and were thrown into prison because you had nothing to pay, how would you feel? Then how would you feel if someone came along and paid your debt?

No doubt you would feel a lifelong indebtedness to that person. And you should. Well, that is what Jesus did for you. Realizing this produces a love relationship with Jesus Christ. Obedience becomes a joy instead of a duty. Naturally, you are concerned lest your new relationship with Christ be severed. But you can find the answer to that by walking close to God.

It is a marvel too that now you are adopted by God as a son—far above a servant. Why then do we talk about service? Because a son that loves his father wants to please him. What pleases the heavenly Father? What is His purpose for His sons? Is it to loaf and loiter their way to heaven? Of course not!

Ephesians 2:8, 9 points out that we are saved by grace, through faith and not by works. Some people stop reading there and sit back. But that is not the end of the thought. Note the next verse. "For we are his workmanship, created in Christ Jesus *unto good works, which God hath before ordained that we should walk in them.*" That is not just duty. It is a privilege. After God has done His wonderful work in you, you find meaning in life by working for Him.

You might ask what happens to the old nature. Is it dead and gone forever? No. At conversion its power is broken and it is, as the Bible calls it, crucified. From that time on, you deny its desires and treat it as dead. Paul said in Galatians 2:20, "I am crucified with Christ: nevertheless I live; yet not I, but Christ liveth in me: and the life which I now live in the flesh I live by the faith of the Son of God, who loved me, and gave himself for me."

What God can make of sinful people is a marvel. If we accept what He says we are and by faith claim the provision He has made, it becomes ours. We must reject and surrender all the rights and desires of our sinful nature and willingly subject ourselves to His will. The decision to do this is the most important and far-reaching decision anybody can ever make. And it can be done in a moment.

The new birth is just the beginning of your spiritual experience, just as your physical birth was just the beginning. Then you needed to grow to live. That is why we must go on to the next chapter to see what it takes to thrive and grow strong spiritually.

Chapter 6

What You Need to Do

You don't have to be a mechanic to drive a car. Most of us who drive don't know exactly what happens in the ignition when we turn the key. We can't explain all the research and engineering that went into the design of the carburetor. Nor does it matter a great deal.

But there are some things we must know to drive a car safely. We have to know how to judge distances so that we can pass a slow-moving truck safely. We must know how to use our mirrors, how to shift gears, and so on. We don't turn the car over to a ten-year-old boy, because he has neither the information nor the maturity to drive. He just doesn't have what it takes.

The Christian life is like that too. In order for Christianity to work in your life, there are some things God expects you to know. And then there are some things God expects you to do. Christianity, if we dare compare it to a new car, is in perfect "working order." Everyone can be saved. Why then aren't all men saved? It's not God's fault. People did not know or do what it takes to have it work in their lives.

Sometimes people know what it takes to come to Christ

in the right way. They may even start out right. Later, however, difficulty comes because they slack off. They seem to forget that, like a car, the Christian life won't work unless you work it.

Understand now, we are not talking about earning salvation by good works. We are talking about the ifs God has laid down, the conditions we must meet so that salvation can work in our hearts and lives. And when we do meet these conditions, we can be assured of a good relationship with God.

One thing everyone must do is

Face the Past

Hasn't the past life caused us enough problems? Shouldn't we want to get away from the past? Finally, yes. But first we must face it and deal with it so that we can put it forever behind us.

To face your past guilt, as you have often heard, you must repent. But what is that? I raise the question because there are many people who do not seem to understand what repentance is.

Some people seem to think that repentance means to say an over-the-shoulder "I'm sorry" and then go their merry way. To them, making some kind of response at an evangelistic meeting, or even going through some kind of instruction meeting and becoming a church member is repentance. But there is much more to it than that! We must go to the Bible to find out what it really is. Then sin can be taken care of in a way that it is gone forever.

Repentance means taking responsibility for your actions and admitting your guilt, not excusing it. You must realize that sin is defiance against God and is worthy of eternal

47

punishment. You must plead for mercy instead of justice. It is said that when the old Puritan, Thomas Hooker, lay dying, friends around his bedside said, "Brother Hooker, you are going to receive your reward." "No, no!" he replied. "I go to receive mercy!"

Repentance also means that instead of enjoying the thought of sin, you must hate it. After all, sin is the cause of your predicament. Hating sin means both being sorry for sin and planning not to do it again. Really meaning business about this produces a complete turnaround.

Until you face your past penitently, God cannot forgive you. But, praise His Name, when you do, God promises to forgive. Listen to His promise: "If we confess our sins, he is faithful and just to forgive us our sins, and to cleanse us from all unrighteousness" (1 John 1:9).

Now the past can be the past. The Bible says in Hebrews 10:17, "And their sins and iniquities will I remember no more." The conscience is clear. The slate is clean, and God allows you to start over.

God forgives. And we must forgive ourselves and go on. Yes, we may be ashamed of how we failed. But by faith we can rejoice in God's forgiveness and forget the past.

But what about restitution? Must restitution be made for everything one has ever done? In most cases that is hardly possible. You can't remember all the wrong things you have ever done. Neither can anyone else. Does forgiveness depend on restitution?

God grants forgiveness because of repentance. Part of repentance is to be willing to make restitution where necessary. But you do not need to be tense and to worry that God might be holding something against you that you have forgotten. God is faithful. Where He wants you to make restitution, He will lay conviction on your conscience. He will remind you to correct things with a person you have lied to or stolen from or hurt in some other way. Don't shrug that responsibility off, because peace of heart will go along with it.

Some young men become overly sensitive in the matter of restitution and confession. Instead of freedom, there is misery. We'll touch this problem in a later chapter.

Now that we have looked at facing the past, we can look at the moment of choice and see what it takes to

Turn Around

You have repented and are willing to make restitution. What next? Actually, at the moment you truly repent, several other things also need to take place.

You trust Christ to forgive you. That is what faith is all about. It's not mysterious. It's simply a matter of believing that Jesus indeed provided forgiveness through His death. Simple as it is, faith is very important. Hebrews 11:6 says, "But without faith it is impossible to please him: for he that cometh to God must believe that he is, and that he is a rewarder of them that diligently seek him."

You forgive others. God has conditioned His forgiveness of our sin upon our forgiveness of others. We pray in the Lord's Prayer, "And forgive us our debts, as we forgive our debtors." Jesus said, "For if ye forgive men their trespasses, your heavenly Father will also forgive you: but if ye forgive not men their trespasses, neither will your Father forgive your trespasses." (See Matthew 6:12–15.)

True repentance makes one realize how greatly he has sinned. This understanding produces a willingness to forgive those who have wronged us. God does not allow us to hold grudges and ill will toward others. Instead, His love in our hearts enables us to love them.

You surrender your will. When General Grant besieged Vicksburg during the Civil War, the fort commanders sent word to him asking the terms of surrender. Grant replied, "Immediate and unconditional surrender!" Naturally, people don't like to surrender so completely as that. But God requires just that. He knows very well that we will try to save one or two habits or attitudes for ourselves unless we have first completely surrendered absolutely everything to Him.

God will not force you to surrender to Him. But when you do, you can no longer set the terms and be the master of your life. Whenever what you want conflicts with what God wants, there is only one way to go—God's way.

Sometimes people try to bargain with God. They are willing to give up a bit, but to give up everything is too much. So they bump along, trying to please both God and their flesh. But it never works, because God and the flesh are pulling in opposite directions. Trying to serve both masters produces unnecessary conflict and frustration.

Surrendering the will is not a once-and-done affair. True, it starts with an initial act. But it must be lived out, day after day. And that is where a problem can start. It's like a child I saw putting money into the offering plate. Just as the plate left, she grabbed to get her coin back. Continuing in a surrendered state year after year tests the sincerity of your surrender.

You may be thinking, "How can I know if I have surrendered?" After the following illustration, I want to ask you one simple test question. A motorcycle club resisted a new law demanding all cycle riders to wear helmets. A spokesman for the group explained, "It's not that we mind wearing helmets. We just don't want to be told to wear them."

Now the question: Do you resent being told what to do? Is there any of the cycle-group spirit in you? Maybe you are tempted to be resentful toward parents, the church, or whatever authority is over you. True surrender submits in a cheerful way. Stubbornness that shows in reluctance or resistance will defeat you if you do not defeat it.

Remember, this is the point that makes or breaks you spiritually. You simply cannot prosper and be strong without surrender. The unsurrendered man thinks strength comes by stiffening his will; but actually, strength comes by surrender to God. Then He can have His mighty way in your heart. And that is real strength!

You commit yourself—the fourth thing that happens at the moment you are converted. Commitment means promising to be loyal to God. It amounts to giving yourself to Him—all you are or ever hope to be. You promise to own Him as master from here on.

The value of commitment shows up best during a severe trial. When you must make a hard decision, you may face confusion and temptation. What should you do? Satan makes many suggestions. Commitment can be the saving factor, because it means you have already settled the question of your loyalties. Because of this, it is not nearly so hard to know what to do because you are committed to follow the Lord.

For example, if you decide ahead of time that you will not become angry the next time something or someone upsets you, you have already won half the battle. For instance, one of your friends may misquote you and make you look bad. What do you do? Commitment has already settled the question; you will not yield and become angry! Commitment looks for the way out that God has promised—and takes it. See 1 Corinthians 10:13 for God's promise.

The good news is that there is another side to commitment. God not only asks us to commit ourselves to Him; He makes a commitment to us. Paul said, "For I know whom I have believed, and am persuaded that he is able to keep that which I have committed unto him against that day." Isn't it wonderful that the one to whom we must commit ourselves has committed Himself to keep our souls safe until that final day?

Repentance, faith, surrender of the will, and commitment are the essence of your part in salvation. They naturally produce obedience to God and a life that is according to the Bible. You can't get along without them. They will serve you well. In conclusion, after turning around, you must

Keep Traveling

You really need nothing new to keep traveling. All you need is more of the same sincerity day after day. Surrender and submission must stay current and fresh. Faith must be kept warm and vibrant. Loving commitment must live as long as you live.

My primary concern here is that you prepare yourself mentally for a long journey. Some people are like meteors in the night and soon burn out and go back to their old ways. The Bible tells us that is worse than not starting at all. You don't want that to happen to you.

Walking with the Lord is the most rewarding thing we can ever do. God is eager to have us trust in Him and treasures our love and loyalty. When you do what it takes on your part, you will gain much more from the Lord than you ever gave up. It's your move. Don't miss it.

Chapter 7

Know Your God

Young man, the country you are traveling through is unknown to you. You are going to need help (and lots of it) to make it to glory safely. No one of us older ones can always be by your side and give you everything it takes. And even if we could always be there, we have our limitations and could not guarantee to be all you will need.

But knowing God is better than knowing the kindest, richest, most powerful person you could name. He is in a better position to help you than any man could ever be. It is extremely important that you develop a thorough acquaintance with Him. And since He is such a great God, it will take all of time and eternity to do that!

Sometimes people say, "It's not what you know but who you know." That is especially true when it comes to knowing God. If you know Him, you can trust Him for what you don't know. When we travel in airplanes, we don't need to know how to fly them, because that is the pilot's job. While we *hope* the pilot knows what he is doing, we don't need to wonder about God; He does.

Some people know a lot about God in the same way we

can know about George Washington and Abraham Lincoln—by hearing or reading about them. These people may have many nice things to say about God, yet they do not know Him personally. To them, God is a force out there somewhere whom they hope to make peace with somehow, sometime. Most of them prefer not to think too seriously about meeting God personally, because it is unnerving. They have no way of knowing how the whole thing will work out.

Other people are quite heathenish about God. Heathens have angry gods. These people are sure that God is just waiting to catch them doing something wrong so that He can pounce on them and do away with them. Whenever something bad happens, they are sure it is from this mean God. (When Hurricane Agnes flooded the eastern part of the United States in 1972, two people were overheard talking. One said, "This was certainly an act of God." The other replied, "I wouldn't know who else to blame.")

Then there are those who say God is all love and goodness. They say that such a loving God could never pour out judgment on those who reject Him. They say that everybody will somehow be saved. That leaves them free to do as they please, because somehow it will all work out. "We're all going to the same place!" they say.

Some people know God is right, but they see only His justice and punishment. They are sure they can't measure up to this holy, austere God. They live in paralyzing fear of impending judgment. You can imagine their misery.

Who is your God? How can you have a comfortable and meaningful relationship with Him? In this chapter we could use many figures of speech to describe our relationship to Him, but we will limit ourselves to just two main ones. First, you need to

Know Him as Sovereign

To be sovereign is to be subject to no one. Nebuchadnezzar is a good illustration. He set people up and put them down at will. He feared no one. Nebuchadnezzar would have agreed with Solomon, who said, "Where the word of a king is, there is power: and who may say unto him, What doest thou?"

And yet Nebuchadnezzar himself finally said of God, "*He* doeth according to his will in the army of heaven, and among the inhabitants of the earth: and none can stay his hand, or say unto him, What doest thou?"

God does all this because he has created everything in the whole universe. Because He has created people, He has the right to dictate how people should behave. He also will judge every man according to those terms. If you lose sight of this, you will become careless and end up doing things that He will not overlook.

God is like parents who accept no nonsense. If you are respectful and obedient, you are on good terms and all is well. But if you violate the rules, you are in trouble. The very same parent who was so kind and loving suddenly becomes someone you need to fear.

Really, the paragraph you have just read describes two different kinds of fear. One kind is respectful fear—the fear to do wrong. Sometimes we call this kind of attitude toward God "reverential fear." The other kind is the chilling fear that the convicted sinner has of God. If we always have and live by the first kind of fear, we won't need to finally face God with dread.

Since God is sovereign, we have no right to become demanding or bossy with Him. We may not blame Him for what we do not understand. We must remember that because

He created us we are His property, and He is not ours.

This might sound negative. It isn't. It is laying the conditions on which you can have a good relationship with Him and can

Know Him as Father

God wants more than just to save you from sin. He wants to mend the father–child relationship that was broken in the Garden of Eden. Before Adam and Eve sinned, they enjoyed walking and talking with Him. When you accept the plan of salvation, you can enjoy walking and talking with Him too.

When God saves people, He takes them, not as servants, but as sons and daughters. So now it's your business (and pleasure) to get to know Him as your personal Father. Regardless of how faithful your earthly father has been to you, your heavenly Father will be much more than that to you.

But, like any other friendship, it has to be kept alive. The son who writes home only when he needs money has a much different relationship with his father than the son who calls his father every day, just to talk. Too many people only call on God when they are in trouble—as if He were a spare tire.

Surely God wants to help you. But He also wants to have a personal relationship with you. He wants to be adored for who He is, not just for what He possesses. I have been told that some of the richest people are the loneliest people because others just want to use them. God must know just how they feel!

God also wants you to feel His love and interest toward you. When things are going well, He wants you to take time to think, "God did that because He loves me." And if you fail? Well, recently a friend of mine was complaining to his wife about a mistake he had made, and she said, "I love you just as much—maybe even a little more, since you need it just now." That idea comes from God; He was the first person to ever feel like that.

But God has provided for you so that you need not fail. Here is the promise: "There hath no temptation taken you but such as is common to man: but God is faithful, who will not suffer you to be tempted above that ye are able; but will with the temptation also make a way to escape, that ye may be able to bear it" (1 Corinthians 10:13). So you know you can count on Him.

And do not think, even in your worst moments, that maybe you aren't worth bothering about. If God cared enough to send Jesus to die for you, He's not going to let you become stranded halfway home. Listen to this: "He that spared not his own Son, but delivered him up for us all, how shall he not with him also freely give us all things?"

At times, fathers need to give correction. So does God. In fact, the Bible says, "For whom the Lord loveth he chasteneth, and scourgeth every son whom he receiveth." That is strong medicine. But if the Lord would refrain, our spiritual result would be the same as for a child who is never spanked. God wants no spoiled children!

Sometimes God's chastening comes through the pricking our own conscience gives us. Or it may come in the form of a rebuke from a parent or church leader. Sometimes God simply lets us bring punishment on ourselves. If you drive carelessly, you might end up in the ditch. God is not obliged to underwrite everything we do.

But remember that God always deals with His own

children for their good. As a young boy, when your parents punished you, you probably found it difficult to appreciate it. But what about now? You have changed your mind considerably, haven't you? Many young men will even say, "I'm glad for every bit of it, and more of it probably wouldn't have hurt me."

The Bible tells us it is those who gracefully accept the chastening hand of God that get the benefit. Those that resent it and blame God rather than love Him lose the blessing they could have gotten from the pain. And if they persist in doing wrong, they lose their relationship with God.

Much of what we discuss in this book deals with practical ways you can learn to know God better. At this point, let's concentrate on the importance of really knowing God in the heart, not just knowing *about* Him. There is a vast difference. When He is in your heart, your friends will know it. They will see it in your actions and reactions, especially in your little, unconscious ones. They will hear it in the tone of your talk. They will see the fruit of the Spirit flowing out of your heart when you have Him within.

Getting to know God is a lifetime of adventure. It is the true joy of living. Young man, fear Him, but then make Him your best friend. He will never let you down.

Chapter 8

Developing Respectable Character

Good character is like steel in a concrete structure. You can't see the steel reinforcement in the concrete, but without it the concrete is weak. A bridge or a building without it would crumble and fall apart under pressure.

Character is not what a person says or pretends to be. It's what he really is beneath the surface. It's what he is in the dark, or when no one is looking, or when the pressure is on. It's what he does by habit. It's what he does when he must decide between right and wrong. It's his main frame—what holds him up and holds him together.

Young man, for you to end right, your character must have steel in it. Without it you will be wishy-washy and too weak to face the battles of life. You would be like a man I worked with who had a drinking problem. When things went well, he could leave the bottle alone. He would even say he hated the stuff and was through with it. But then something would happen—like the day he got into a hassle with his in-laws. Where do you think he went? Back to the bottle and back on everything he had said. When the going became difficult, he was powerless.

You don't need to be like that. While you probably wouldn't be tempted to go for the bottle, you do not need to be defeated in areas where you *are* tempted. If your character has steel in it, you can be successful even in times of trial and testing.

Good character cannot be bought, but neither is it free. It won't come walking to you. No one can give it to you, or even force it on you, no matter how much they might wish they could. Even your parents and their teachings can't produce it in you.

Let me try to explain

What Produces Your Character

Character is produced by the principles that you allow to rule your life. It's not the good teaching you hear but what you do with it that produces good character. It's not what you talk about but what you put into practice in your everyday living.

What you practice, you will become. If you live nobly, you will have noble character. If you live selfishly, your character will be selfish. If you live carelessly and lazily, your character will become just that.

Some young men have had very little good teaching and yet have strong, solid character. Their lives glow with goodness even though the circumstances they grew up in were very difficult and discouraging. That is because they chose to do right as far as they knew, even though the place they were in made it hard to do so. Many a young man who was strong for God started in such a place.

Then there are those young men (and some who are now old) whose parents worked hard and well to train them, even agonizing over them—only to see them become moral and spiritual disasters. Although we don't know all the reasons, we can be sure that the young men's own attitudes were a major part of the outcome. This explains in part why one brother in a family can turn out right and another in the same family can turn out so poorly.

So, young man, your character is largely the result of your choices. While training has its impact, you decide what that training will do to you. To have good character, you must choose to have it.

But the power of choice does not perform any magic. Determination and self-discipline are not enough. Even being born again does not automatically bestow on you a whole set of desirable character traits. It will give you the desire and the power to have a good character, but you must let God put you through His character-refining school for many years to complete the work.

Character has as many sides as a diamond. We will talk about some of them individually. First we'll look at *honesty* because it is

God's Handle on a Man

If a man is not honest, it's hard to reason with him, because he won't face the facts. He always makes excuses and wiggles out of his responsibilities. God Himself can't help a man who will not admit that he does anything wrong.

The biggest problem lies not in saying that black is white. Rather, it is in shading the facts to make things easier for ourselves. You know how tempting it is not to give all the facts if it makes it harder for you or costs you more money.

The conductor of a stalled train was supposed to warn an oncoming train of the danger ahead. He ran back waving his lantern, but the next train kept coming and crashed violently into the first one. When brought before the judge, he gave his story. He was exonerated because he had waved his lantern. Afterwards he confided with a sigh of relief, "I'm sure glad no one asked me if the lantern was lit!"

Young men who say, "I don't know," "I don't remember," "I'm not sure," "Maybe I did," and the like sound just like that signal man.

Practically the same thing is shifting blame. Adam blamed Eve. Eve blamed the serpent. You can do the same by making remarks like, "It was your idea," or "If he hadn't done it, I wouldn't have either."

Befogging the truth never solves anything. It compounds the trouble. The truth is always the least painful and the most rewarding. Even more, it is just plain right. Anything less than the truth will only burden your conscience.

Now let me make a few practical points.

Don't sell the truth, even if it seems like a small thing. A bank was about to promote a young man to a place of high responsibility. One lunchtime a bank director happened to be a short distance behind him in the cafeteria line-up. He saw the young man slyly cover his butter with other food so that the cashier could not see it. He lost his integrity for a sliver of butter. He also lost his promotion and his job.

Keep your commitments. If you agree to do a job for a certain amount, don't turn around and take another for more money until you have finished the first one. If you say you will pay on Thursday, don't wait until Friday. If you say you will meet someone at a certain time, you need to do all you can to be there on time. Of course, developments beyond your control can change your plans. But don't become known as one of those people who is always late.

Cultivate a sensitive conscience. If you always honor it,

then anytime you start to slip into dishonesty, your conscience will blow the whistle. But if you don't honor it, your
conscience will become hardened and let you lie all you want.
Finally you will believe your own lies. How will God be able
to get hold of you then? At that point, it will be very difficult for God to help you see yourself and your needs.

But recognize a supersensitive conscience if you have
one. If you tell a friend that your father is baling hay, and
later you find out he was fixing the baler, have you told a
lie? Of course not, if you said what you thought was the
truth. Can you say you read a book if you aren't sure you
read every word? Can you say it's half past eight if the clock
really says it's 8:28? Usually the answer is yes. God wants
us to be truthful and comfortable at the same time.

Now for the next trait. *Dependability* is

A Real Trust Winner

Being dependable touches every area of your life, not
just work. Can your parents depend on you to act right when
out of their sight? Pardon me for asking; it's just that some
young men seem to need to have this question put to them
as if they were ten years younger.

Can others depend on you to stick up for what is right?
Or do you just go along with whomever you are with? Can
you resist pressure and fun making in order to do right?

If you aren't home at the expected time, can your parents
trust you to have a good reason? Or do you leave them guess-
ing why you have been careless about getting home and what
your excuse will be this time? Sometimes young people say,
"My parents don't trust me!" Remember that trust is earned.
Be worthy of it, and in most cases you will get it.

At work, do you follow instructions? Or do you take it on

yourself to do as you think? Many times the boss doesn't give all his reasons for wanting things done a certain way. Perhaps if you are told to use the Dodge pickup instead of the Ford, it's because the Ford has no brakes or no license.

Change the directions you get only when you are sure those over you would want a change if they knew what you know. A man dying of cancer told his wife he thought it best not to have a public viewing after his death because his face was extremely thin and unpleasant to see. But when his widow saw how well the funeral director had done in making her husband's face look healthy and natural again, she hardly knew what to do. Should she do what she had agreed to do or what she knew her husband would want if he knew? She finally decided to allow a public viewing.

You need to be dependable, not only to make it in society and in the workplace, but in order to make it spiritually. Little things like getting up on time in the morning and being prompt and thorough in your duties will prepare you for greater responsibilities. Jesus tells us, "He that is faithful in that which is least is faithful also in much: and he that is unjust in the least is unjust also in much" (Luke 16:10). Colossians 3:23 adds, "And whatsoever ye do, do it heartily, as to the Lord, and not unto men."

Young man, can the Lord depend on you? If He can, others can too. They will have much for you to do.

Chapter 9

Developing Generous Character

Most people look out for themselves first. Only a few are generous by nature. If you are one of those few, be glad of it. But for the rest of us, generosity is a character trait that we must develop.

Let's think first about selfishness in other people. (It is easier to see it in others than in ourselves.) Do you enjoy being with people who expect others to do more than they would think of doing? Or who are generous only when generosity doesn't interfere with their own wants and comforts? Or who, whenever they are a little generous, expect to be praised for it? Can you imagine what this world would be like if *everyone* belonged to the "me generation"?

Now we will look at it from the positive angle and think about

Unselfishness

Unselfishness is being more interested in others than in ourselves. I almost said "forgetting about ourselves." That would be very difficult, of course. But the greater our love and concern for others, the closer we come to that. In fact, unselfishness is at the heart of effective service to God and others. Would Jesus have done what He did if He had been selfish? Or Paul, or any person who was useful to God?

Now it is true that some people are unselfish for selfish reasons. They give because they expect more back. There was a pastor who had that kind of member in his congregation. This member would ceremoniously give his pastor a gift each year. But when the day came that the pastor needed to deal with some faults in this member's life, the gifts stopped.

Some people give to make others debtors to them. They keep a mental ledger of IOUs which they expect to collect—along with something extra too! Meanwhile, they bask in their supposed generosity. They are a lot like the Pharisees who rattled their money into the offering box.

Being good just for recognition can be a snare. You know how it feels to want others to know about the good you do. Were you ever tempted to fold a dollar bill tighter than a twenty-dollar bill when you put it in the offering? That's really a form of selfishness.

Unselfishness is doing good for good's sake—not for personal advantage. It is wanting to serve and not be served. A president said it well in his inaugural address: "Ask not what your country can do for you; ask what you can do for your country." Winston Churchill calling Britain to action said, "I have nothing to offer but blood, toil, tears, and sweat." He was calling his fellow Englishmen to look out for their country before they looked out for themselves. Such patriotism may be noble in an earthly way. But the Christian has a far more noble reason than that to forget himself. He serves Jesus Christ and His people.

You might think you want to be unselfish but don't get

the opportunity. You haven't been involved in some daring rescue in which flames licked a gas tank three feet from your head. No one has ever asked you to make a great sacrifice. You haven't come across any Goliaths to kill.

The fact is, unselfishness starts in the normal course of life. Remember that David was made ready to face Goliath by faithfully tending his father's sheep. It was a thankless, lonely job. But his steadiness there prepared him for the lion, the bear, and eventually Goliath.

You might not see opportunities to be unselfish, because you see them only for other people. Try to see yourself as other people see you; maybe you will see more ways to be unselfish that way.

The amazing thing is that unselfish people usually don't see themselves at all, or hardly at all. They don't seem to realize they are being unselfish. To them, it is a way of life. A need comes up, and there is no question but that they do what they can to relieve it.

While I was writing this book, a grizzly bear attacked two brothers in our area. The one got away, but the grizzly pounced on the other one. Instead of deserting his brother and running away, the free man went right up to the bear with his gun to avoid the risk of hitting his brother and shot the bear. When praised for his bravery, he shrugged and said, "You do what has to be done."

In Matthew 25, Jesus told of those who had done many sacrificial things. But, when praised for it, they wondered when they had done them. It was so normal and a part of them that it never occurred to them that it was noteworthy. But it was to God.

Normally, unselfishness isn't glamorous. And you had better forget about always being recognized for it. Jesus told of a servant who had worked hard all day, then in the evening had to serve his master before he could eat. Was such a servant to be complimented for his unselfish service? Jesus answered with a no. Instead, He said that after we have done everything we can, we are to say it was our duty. No honor, no recognition, nothing—just an admission of duty accomplished.

A man came to the scene of an accident where a person was pinned in the vehicle. He exerted himself tremendously in twisting metal to free the injured person. While he was fading back into the crowd, someone wanted to put the spotlight on him. He shrugged, saying, "It was nothing. Someone was hurting, so I helped."

The unselfish heart is touched as if the other person's needs were its own. But self-interest deadens the heart's ability to care about others. The priest and the Levite in the parable of the Good Samaritan were too full of themselves to be touched by the plight of the poor man who fell among the thieves. It was the generous Samaritan who opened his heart. That's why he is called good. Jesus made his act immortal by holding him up as an example of real love.

Young man, how is it with you? Do you get more satisfaction out of pleasing others than yourself? Can you change your plans for the sake of others—even for a little brother? Are you troubled a bit when you realize you have not responded to the needs of others? Be glad if you are, and do better the next time!

There is actually a satisfaction in ignoring yourself for the sake of others. The more we do that, the richer and broader life becomes. That's what Jesus meant when He said, "It is more blessed to give than to receive." Those who are wrapped up in themselves make a mighty small package. And they aren't happy either.

There is another inseparable companion of unselfishness, called

Helpfulness

Did you ever hear of the fellow who said work fascinates him? He could sit and watch it all day. He may have been first cousin to the man who spent a week with an acquaintance of ours. Right away he announced he was on vacation and planned to take it easy. He did—at the expense of his host. I suspect his friends did not mourn his departure.

On the other hand, friends visiting me have often helped out tremendously—sometimes at things they were especially handy at. I've often been glad to have a willing mechanic or carpenter around. Others have gladly worked at jobs they weren't especially handy at, and I appreciated that too.

Someone once said, "Everybody who comes makes us happy—some when they come, and some when they go." You know which type you want to be.

A helpful person tries to avoid making things inconvenient for others. When he sees a need, he does what he can about it. And he doesn't wait until he is asked.

Naturally, if you are sick or hurt, you can't always take care of yourself. That's no disgrace. But when able-bodied people enjoy being waited on hand and foot, something noble is missing.

Clean up after yourself. The person using the bathroom after you leave it should find it ready to use. Once I saw a sign posted in a factory that said, "Clean up after yourself. Your mother doesn't work here." Well, where your mother does work, cleaning up after yourself is just as important.

It isn't beneath your dignity to give a hand at the dishes

now and then or to do some odd jobs around the house. A married man visiting his parents pointed out to his younger brother that the refrigerator door swung open because the refrigerator needed to be leveled. The next time he came, the refrigerator was level—thanks to a helpful young man in the house!

Sometimes young men think they have outgrown helping with little things. Really, it's just the opposite. The more they grow, the sharper their eyes ought to be for little ways to be helpful. Don't act as if home is a motel and restaurant. Likewise, at work, don't try to see how little you can get by with. Some people work harder to stay out of work than they would have had to work to do it. The men who do more than their share, not surprisingly, get the most pleasure out of their jobs.

In our area there are two sawmills whose production per man is vastly different. In one mill, the employees are constantly quarreling with the management about wages, work conditions, and benefits. The management, in turn, threatens to shut the mill down.

In the other mill, the day shift and the night shift compete with each other to see which can saw the most wood. One employee told me that at break time they study the production report of the other shift. If they are behind, he said, they really fly into the work. In fact, the management had to slow them down for cost-efficiency reasons. Which mill do you think would be the more pleasant place to work?

The same is true in church life. If the lawn needs to be mowed or the building needs to be painted, be there. Don't hesitate to volunteer. Make helpfulness a habit. That way others will know they can count on you when they need help. About three years ago a close friend of mine passed away.

You know, I still find myself thinking of him when I need a hand, because he was always so helpful.

Give more than you get. Amazingly, you will discover that you are getting back more than you gave. It's a good way to live.

Be careful not to do things just for recognition from people. Do it for the Lord. He will take it that way. And you will have another solid virtue in your pursuit of strong character.

Chapter 10

Developing a Respectful Character

Give yourself a little test. Identify the persons with respectful character.

"Such a slow driver!" Clyde jammed on the brakes. "Pokey old man. He acts as if he has all day." Clyde swerved close to the man's rear bumper as he swung out to pass.

Frank hurried toward the supermarket door. There was an old man limping toward it too. Frank opened the door and patiently waited for the old man to pass through first.

"Why don't you come with us tonight?" asked Harry.
"My father said I am to stay home tonight," Sam answered.
"What?" Harry shot back. "If my dad told me to stay home, I'd . . ."

Richard laughed. "Did you see that man on the other side of the street? He walked like this."

John joined the other young men after church. The conversation ended abruptly. Lester winked at Mike, and they both burst out laughing.

Calvin nudged Aaron and pushed a note at him. Aaron paid no attention but kept on listening to the minister. Calvin folded his arms and slid a little lower into his seat.

"There's the town drunk. He's such a bum," Curtis said. "But he has a soul, just like you and I," answered Wayne.

A rather easy quiz, wasn't it? As soon as you see them described in print, it's obvious who is respectful and who isn't. Respect appears so attractive and disrespect so disgusting that it seems almost strange then that any young men should have to be told about these things.

But as obvious as respect and disrespect may be to the onlooker, we can't deny that these young men faced real temptations. In some cases, doing right meant going against the group they were with. Maybe ignorance or thoughtlessness caused some of the wrong responses. However the case may be, these illustrations are true enough to experience to show that being respectful is a character trait that has to be worked at.

Sometimes it seems that being disrespectful is a special temptation to young men. Why is this so? Is disrespect supposed to be a way of showing independence or of being grown-up? Or is it because in some circles it is considered the "in" thing to do? Surely it is not too difficult for you to see that manliness and mannerliness are the marks of maturity, not crudeness and rudeness. And while disrespect may be the "in" thing with a certain set of young people, it is certainly the "out" thing with God.

Your respect or lack of it shows your whole system of values. How you treat others shows what you think of them. The way you act shows what you think of God—and what you think of yourself. Sometimes you may need to respect others not so much because they deserve it but because you want to be respectable.

We certainly can't touch all the areas of life that involve respect in this chapter. What we will do is pick out a few of the basic ones. If you take these seriously, it will help you know how to handle the ones that are not mentioned.

First there must be

Respect for God

No question about it, God is worthy of respect. Being the Creator, Sustainer, and Judge of the universe, He is entitled to it. Man must admit his smallness when compared to God.

But too often people treat God with gross disrespect. Is this because God does not immediately punish those who disrespect Him? Or perhaps because He seems far away? Certainly it's no more reasonable to disrespect God than to disrespect an employer whom you can't see. What does it matter if your employer has moved away? He still quite logically expects you to respect his word—and not only that, but also his property and the people he has left in charge. God, like that employer, measures our respect for Him by how we treat His people and His Word.

Accepting authority can be a major test for a young man. You may have had surges of feeling that it's about time for you to be your own boss. That time will come, but not by your resisting authority.

Since God is the source of all authority, anyone who disrespects his boss, his preacher, his father, or the local policeman disrespects God. Can you disrespect your foreman without disrespecting the employer who put him in charge? Of course not! Can you disrespect your employer without disrespecting God? No again. As Paul said in Romans, "Whosoever therefore resisteth the power, resisteth the ordinance of God: and they that resist shall receive to themselves damnation."

Respecting God means respecting His Word. This means not scoffing at acts of obedience such as practicing the ordinances. There is more than one young (or once young) man who used to laugh at those who sincerely obeyed the Bible and is now lost in the world. Why? No one can ever mock God's Word and escape terrific loss of conscience. Even the Book itself should be handled with special care. This is part of showing respect to God.

Reverence in worship services is a part of respect for God. Surely you know enough to be quiet, to help sing, and to listen when the Word is preached. But perhaps you haven't thought that these are ways to show respect to God. Furthermore, the *way* you sing and the *way* you listen make a big difference. Congregations that love to praise the Lord have quite a different feel from congregations that "just sing." As to listening to the sermon, don't forget that if you can see the preacher, he can see you too. He knows whether you take notes and give an occasional little smile or nod, or whether you sit there with a faraway look in your eyes. You'd be surprised how much you encourage or discourage a minister by the way you listen!

A young man was once complaining how boring and dry the church service had been. His grandfather, who had observed him during the service, explained to him why he had been bored. The young man had come to church, slouched down in his seat, and done very little to get involved. No wonder he thought the service was dull! The dullness was in his own heart and mind. And because he put nothing into the service, he got nothing out of it.

How do you handle the person next to you who wants to whisper or show you pictures during the service? Just shake your head at him or ask him to tell you after church. If you've ever had someone do that to you, you know that you respected him for his courage and conviction even though you didn't appreciate it at the time.

We all understand that church leaders are God's men, chosen by Him and working for Him. But what if they make mistakes? The fact is, they don't claim to be perfect. If God required us to respect only people who do everything right, the world's whole system of authority would collapse. Just remember that in a few years you will be sitting in a place of authority—you probably have some authority (or influence) among the younger people now—and you know you will need some forbearing from people under you.

The Bible teaches us in Romans 13:1–3 to respect our civil government. "Let every soul be subject . . ." This includes the president and congressmen. (Someone once said, "To hear my relatives talk, you'd think the people running the country are the dumbest in the world, and that I have the smartest relatives in the world.") The responsibility to respect civil leaders extends all the way down to the local tax collector and the borough policeman.

And don't think the officers of the law don't know what the Bible teaches. They have a pretty good idea, and they expect Christians to live up to their Book. Visitors to our church one Sunday were stopped afterwards by a policeman for not fastening their seat belts. The driver frankly admitted, "Yes, we know about the seat belt law. When we crossed the border into the province, we saw a sign telling us to buckle up, and we all did. But just now we were leaving church and were busy talking, and we forgot. So—well—we're guilty."

The officer said, "I'll let you go this time. But I'll watch for you in the future. *And,* when you get home, I want you to open your Bibles and read Romans chapter 13, verses 1 to 3!'"

Our next thought could fit under "Respect for God" as well. But because of its importance, we will give it special attention. It is

Respect for Parents

Your parents are the first authority you ever encountered. They are the ones who taught you that you couldn't always have your own way. They trained you to take direction and submit to others.

How you respond to their direction is still important today, and very far-reaching. Normally, the way a young man feels toward his parents is the way he feels toward God. If he refuses his parents' authority, he seldom respects other authority. (That smart aleck in school probably learned to talk that way at home.)

God considers respect for parents important enough that He made it one of the Ten Commandments: "Honour thy father and thy mother." The New Testament repeats it in Ephesians 6:2 and adds in verse 3, "That it may be well with thee." How typical of God—always asking us to do what is best for us in the long run.

Young Man, Be Strong

Both verses start with *honour.* What is that? Is it only exact obedience, and no more? No. Honor reaches much further than that. You can obey without honoring, but you can't honor without obeying.

It works like this example. Your parents expect you not to watch television. But they have never said anything specific about video shows or the theater. Does that make these things permissible then? Of course not! It is wrong because it is not obeying what you know their wishes would be. So don't ever excuse yourself by saying, "Oh, well, they never told me not to do that."

What if your parents don't draw a strong line between right and wrong for you? Suppose they don't care, or even encourage you to do something questionable. Does that release you from responsibility to do what you know you should? I am sure you know the answer to that. Don't yield to the temptation to excuse yourself. Rather, be a help to them by doing what is right even if no one else in your family does.

Another question is whether it is ever right to go against your parents. Your first responsibility is to God. If they or anyone else asks you to go against God's direction, you cannot do it. But you must be careful that the Bible clearly shows you another way.

Respect also affects the way you talk to your parents. Sometimes parents allow their children to talk to them in chilling tones or tell them what to do with never a "please" or a "thank you." Perhaps you are old enough now to know that you could be giving more respect to your parents than they are insisting on. Give it by all means. It will enrich your relationship to your parents more than you believe possible. They will enjoy having you around; you will enjoy them more; and you will be a good example to the other children. Most important, you will have a better relationship with the Lord.

What is your response if your parents do not approve some plans of yours and you are disappointed? Instead of grumbling, sit down and discuss it with your parents. It's all right to ask your parents "why" sometimes. You need to be respectful, but there's a right way to do it. Parents are usually wise enough to recognize a "why" that comes along with a good attitude. Although your parents probably won't change their minds, you will have built something good again into your friendship with them. And no doubt you will profit from looking at the matter from their side.

We'll have to admit that some parents aren't very approachable. But you must be sure that you at least did your part. And if you remember to discuss pleasant subjects with them and not just problems, you might succeed surprisingly well.

Remember that your parents probably won't live as long as you do. Respect them while you can. Flowery speeches and wet Kleenexes after it's too late are as nothing compared to honoring them right now.

Finally, the greatest tribute of respect you can give Christian parents is to respect their God supremely.

The last phase of respect we will discuss is

Respect for Others

Again we'll begin at home. Do you listen when your brothers and sisters talk to you, or are you off in a world of your own? When your younger brother's shoestring tears, and he is getting frustrated because he can't position the knot right, what happens? When he cries because you said, "No,

79

Young Man, Be Strong

I can't go fishing with you today," what happens? (Not that you should give him everything he wants.) When someone picks up a book you laid down for a minute, what happens? Your reactions make a deep impression on your younger brothers and sisters, because they usually admire the older ones. Don't let them down.

Sometimes it is considered "sissy" to be kind, and "grown-up" to be coarse and crude. Nonsense! You wouldn't think it "grown-up" to treat crudely certain people who are special to you. The same consideration applies to your own family.

How do you relate to people your parents' age? Can you talk with them comfortably after church, or must you always be with your own age group? Don't be in a rush to head for the door after church. Wait to talk to some people who are not your age. If they don't notice you, take a deep breath, if you must, and seek them out. When your family goes visiting, you can enjoy sharing with adults. It will enlarge your world immensely.

Sometime take your sister and visit a retirement home. The elderly often don't have access to as much of the world as you do, and they will be glad for your visit. At the same time, they have access to a world you have never known, since they remember things that happened long before you were born. Don't forget to listen! You will receive an education, and the older person will enjoy having you for an audience. You can be of much encouragement to them.

If you live with older people every day, remember little courtesies like holding doors, providing cushioned seats, talking loudly enough, and so on.

Then there are the abnormal and the handicapped. Sometimes you get the feeling they won't know the difference if you stare at them or ignore them altogether. Actually, it's surprising how much they know. Remember their names and say a few words to them when you can.

And help your little brother not to mock or tease a handicapped person. I'm thinking of one family who has a handicapped boy. At an all-day church meeting, this child was surrounded by a group of teasing boys. How painful it must have been!

What causes disrespect? Perhaps it's just not thinking how disrespect feels to others. But more important, it has a lot to do with disrespect toward God. If you respect God properly, you will respect others as well.

As you can see, strong character is very practical. Every part of your life is affected by it. You can not afford to take the "easy road" in any way. As you let God and those around you chisel away at your corners, you can become more and more like God wants you to be.

Good character will serve you well. Treat your character right, and it will treat you right. Developing the traits we have discussed will prepare you for greater development.

To summarize these last three chapters, let's notice

Character Demonstrated

Daniel of the Bible is a good example of much we have been discussing. He was a splendid balance of numerous good traits.

Respectable? Yes. He wouldn't lie even to save his life. He was so dependable in his religion that his enemies knew if they could make his religion a trap, he would be caught. And he didn't let them down. He prayed just as they expected. Are you that dependable?

Generous? Yes. Although he was given important positions,

he never used them selfishly. He always sought the good of others.

Respectful? Yes. Even in a foreign land, he honored his God. No doubt he also was respecting his parents by living up to what they had taught him. He even respected Nebuchadnezzar, with all his strange ways, because God had placed him in power.

Young man, let these principles be the law of your life. Don't even consider living any other way. Determination ahead of time will prepare you to respond to the unexpected and the unknown.

These few traits are not all we could have mentioned. But as you work on these, many more will follow. God bless you as you become strong for Him.

Chapter 11

Four Emotional Pitfalls

Emotions are wonderful. God gave them to us so that we can "feel" the experiences of life. Someone said the emotions help give life a sharp edge. Life would certainly be drab and meaningless if we had no feelings. Healthy emotions enable us to love, to be glad, to be sober, and even to be sad if necessary.

But emotions can also be cruel. If they are not controlled, they become the master rather than the "helper" they are intended to be. Uncontrolled emotions can lead to very serious problems. They affect your whole system—physical, nervous, and mental. Deep depression and even suicide are often related to emotional difficulties.

Such talk about emotions may seem extreme and far from you. But even if you haven't had any difficulty with your emotions, there are those who have. And since we have emotions, we must be concerned that they are our servant and not our master. We are discussing the emotions to help you enjoy them in the way God intends. The chapter title suggests that there are particular pitfalls to watch out for. Before we go into them you need to understand

How Your Emotions Affect You

Emotions (or feelings) are fickle. They can change so quickly. One disappointment, and you can feel as if the world crashed in on you. A compliment, and you can feel elated. Haman, when he left the king's palace after banqueting, was walking on air. But his buoyancy all evaporated when one man refused to bow to him at the gate.

Emotions are unpredictable because they are not tied to facts. You can have a good job and a good family and be right with God, and yet feel as if something is wrong with your life because the day is cloudy or you feel tired.

Emotions are powerful. They will make you feel like working if things go your way. Or they will make you feel like not getting up in the morning if things look a bit dark. They will control you if you let them. Instead of doing what you should, whether you feel like it or not, you can end up doing what you feel like doing, whether you should or not. Sometimes you will have to take your emotions strongly in hand. One man learned that when he found himself thinking, "I don't feel like it," he could also say to himself, "So what? I'll do it anyway."

Emotions set thinking patterns. Have you noticed how easy it is to accept a half-hour wait one day, but the next day the same wait seems like a disaster? Or have you ever started out a day feeling sorry for yourself—and sure enough, all through the day you found reasons to pity yourself?

Controlling emotions is an important part of being strong spiritually. While there are many aspects to emotions, we will discuss only four that can cause trouble if you do not cope with them. The first has to do with the conscience. Good and necessary as the conscience is, it can also be troublesome and affect the emotions. This is especially true when there is the

Problem of an Oversensitive Conscience

Some people's consciences aren't sensitive enough. Such persons can cheat, lie, or steal and not be troubled. On the other hand, some people's consciences work overtime. Even when they repent and apologize for something they have done wrong, they keep wondering if they apologized right.

A young man with this difficulty is almost afraid to feel good about his Christian life for fear he may be overlooking something that God is not pleased about. He is almost afraid to tell a story or say anything for sure, such as, "We are having a rainy summer," or, "It's twenty after eight," lest he find out later that he wasn't quite right. A conscience like this can cause a lot of misery!

When you feel guilty, of course you have to keep in mind that your conscience might be working perfectly well, and you actually have done something wrong. Even an oversensitive conscience is often right. When it is, pay attention to it.

But if your conscience bothers you about things that don't matter or are taken care of, you need to face that and determine what causes your problem.

Perhaps you lack faith. If you confess sin and make whatever restitution is necessary, and still don't feel that God has forgiven you, are you believing God? The temptation to not trust God's forgiveness might seem humble and innocent enough, but it's actually a temptation to sin. Remember, "without faith it is impossible to please him: for he that cometh to God must believe that he is, and that he is a rewarder of them that diligently seek him."

Of course, the oversensitive conscience may argue that

maybe you didn't seek Him quite diligently enough. Well, seeking diligently is important. But finally, we are saved, not by coming to God perfectly, but by trusting God to save us. All the thief on the cross said was, "Lord, remember me when thou comest into thy kingdom." Maybe the thief should have said more. Maybe he could have wondered if he had a perfectly perfect attitude. But he trusted the Lord, and the Lord did the rest.

Keep in mind too that Satan can use arguments that sound ever so logical to prove that your heart is not right with God. The more you resist, the more he persists! Don't ever argue with the devil over a thing you have settled with God. Rather, say, "Get thee behind me, Satan!"—and then go on with life, trusting the Lord rather than allowing your conscience to disturb you.

Of course, the problem might not be that you lack faith. Perhaps your conscience is just naturally more sensitive than other people's. You might be the type who is more exact in following your father's rules than others are. Perhaps your feelings are easily hurt. Remember, then, that your sensitivity can color the world for you like sunglasses or a candy wrapper in front of the eye, which do not always show you life as it really is.

Being with other overly sensitive people too much can make it harder for you. Try to associate with cheerful, level-headed friends who aren't easily bothered by things that don't matter.

Remember that your conscience is not the final authority. "If our heart condemn us, God is greater than our heart, and knoweth all things." What God says in His Word is the final authority, and the conscience is only a channel God uses to touch you. Usually the conscience is quite dependable.

But the Bible must be the "conscience" of your conscience. Only when your conscience fully agrees with the Word of God can it be trusted.

Another way to handle an oversensitive conscience is to seek counsel from people who are spiritually mature. When your mind gets muddled, it can be difficult to really know what is what. Getting help from people you have confidence in will bring relief. The help they give you can also be valuable the next time you face a similar problem.

Finally, trust God with childlike faith. Having faith is an act of the will and not a matter of feeling. Accept the facts given in the Bible and claim them for your own. Believe in God's mercy and goodness to all the repentant. If you are sincere, He will lead you right. If you seek Him with all your heart, you can rest in assurance that God accepts you.

Thank God for your conscience. Treasure it. Treat it right, and it will serve you well. Deal with wrongs you have done when your conscience first begins to prod you about them, so that you can be free in conscience.

Identifying a Superiority Complex

A complex is, as you can see from its name, obviously not simple. It's not like a stone in your shoe that makes you feel irritable. It's a whole set of actions and attitudes that a person might have for a whole set of reasons. And those reasons might be hard to pinpoint.

Someone with a superiority complex thinks, or seems to think, that in looks, intelligence, strength, class, or popularity, no one can measure up to him. He always wants the last word to make it clear who is the greatest.

This attitude shows up in the way he treats others. He can be very critical, or he can "talk down" to others from his lofty height. He sounds a bit the way Goliath must have sounded when he talked to David. He hands out advice freely because, after all, who has more answers? He also can be very sarcastic and belittle others to reinforce his "greatness."

This might not be a problem to you. But it is something to think through, because there are various shades of it, and one of those shades might be yours. Some people are more modest than others but still have a superiority complex. And that involves pride.

Pride doesn't even stand up to reason. Suppose you *are* more quick-witted or even a bit smarter than some others; do you have any right to glory in it? Who gave you your ability? Is it right then to treat even the lowliest condescendingly? The answers are obvious. Since God made us all, no one has a right to take any glory to himself. All glory must go to God. Remember what happened to Herod in Acts 12 when he accepted honor that should have gone to God.

How can you deal with this problem? Label it for the pride it is. It is a characteristic of the old, unconverted man, and it needs to be crucified. For another way of saying it, you need to fall on the Rock, Christ Jesus, and be broken.

Walk close to God. Measure yourself against Him rather than against others. That always produces humility. When measured against God, who would have anything to feel superior about? Regardless of who we are or what we have done, it is only by the grace of God.

The next complex that involves the emotions is supposedly the opposite of the superiority complex.

Understanding the Inferiority Complex

People who feel inferior suffer from the mistaken idea that everybody else is better than they are. Since they think another person can always do a thing better than they can, they are afraid to try. Often they are uncomfortable with other people and prefer not to do or say anything to attract people's eyes toward them. Often too they put other people on pedestals, as one would do with a marble statue. The minister, or certain other people, they seem to think, are "way up there." And they believe that, by thinking this way, they are being humble.

Now real humility can be appreciated, but an inferiority complex is destructive. Often an inferior-feeling person resents the very thoughts he entertains. Although he sees himself as inferior, he doesn't like it. He resents people who are more aggressive or gifted. He pities himself, and neglects to do what he could do. He often "downs" himself, talking about his blunders and forgetfulness and so on. But if anybody agrees with him that he is as inferior as he says, look out!

The story goes that a man said one day, "Well, I may have many faults, but one thing is certain: I am not proud."

An acquaintance said, "Huh, that's easily understood. You have nothing to be proud of."

"What!" said the man. "I have as much to be proud of as you do, or anybody else does!" This goes to show that there might be more pride sticking in a man who acts super-humble than one might have thought.

The inferiority complex is as much a part of the old, unconverted man as pride is. If someone complains about the way he is, he is talking against his Creator. He is saying to God, "Why hast thou made me thus?"

Another way he is damaged by false humility is that he fails to develop the potential he does have. Everybody has some things he can do well. But some people bury those talents

Young Man, Be Strong

because they keep thinking about the talents they don't have.

What should you do if you have these tendencies? Should you read the "I'm somebody" type of book so popular today? Should you go all out to prove to others that you are somebody after all? That is what some psychologists would say.

But there is a better way. Take a God's-eye view. Remember that to God everybody is of equal importance and worth. True, there are different callings and different gifts. But it takes everyone to make the world work. Have you ever heard someone complain, "We have too many leaders and not enough followers"? After all, which are more important?

Remind yourself that you probably don't realize how important everyone really is, which includes yourself. Paul, speaking to the philosophers on Mars' Hill, said, "We are . . . [God's] offspring." Also, being a friend of God as a Christian gives you a special position. Someone has said, "When a king picks up a trifle, it is a trifle no longer."

Also, realize that God seems to see to it that "every prince limps." Everybody has flat sides and areas where he needs to improve. This fact helps to equalize us.

So look at the facts. True humility doesn't see itself as high or low, but just sees itself as it is.

And then forget about how high or low you are. A man once asked a rather oversimplified question: "So we're not supposed to feel humble, and we're not supposed to feel proud. Then how are we supposed to feel?" The answer: Why bother to think about yourself at all?

Accept yourself as God created you. He accepts you, or He wouldn't have made you as you are. He had a special reason for making you the way He did. Walk close to Him, and feel His love. Then your life will be more worthwhile

90

than you once thought it could be.

Dealing With Insecurity

Insecurity—almost everybody has it. Everybody needs some of it. It can be either an asset or a liability, depending on what people do with it. A Christian believer can harness insecurity and make it work for him.

In what ways can insecurity be an asset? It can keep you from being overconfident—which is a real snare. Not being too sure of yourself while driving on the highway can make you a safer driver. Sometimes young men get the idea they are better drivers than they really are. Having enough insecurity to make you cautious, to keep you from following other vehicles too closely, and to slow you down when road conditions are hazardous is to your advantage.

The same caution is effective spiritually. Remember how Peter jumped out of the boat to go to Jesus. His confidence evaporated, and he found himself feeling very insecure. He expressed the same confidence the night before Jesus was crucified when he said, "Though I should die with thee, yet will I not deny thee." That same night he denied the Lord three times. Had he been more cautious and less confident in himself, he would likely have trusted the Lord more.

A measure of insecurity can help make you more sensitive to others who struggle with it because you know what it's like to feel shaky. Then you can encourage them more sympathetically. More than that, healthy insecurity can drive you to the Lord for real security. True humility will be the fruit.

Insecurity becomes a liability when it makes you feel uncomfortable and threatened by circumstances. It can make you feel that others are against you and will take advantage of you at the first opportunity. It can tempt you to take everything people do as a personal offense.

It's almost a contradiction, but sometimes insecure people seem to feel superior. They may put up a bold front to discourage others from challenging them. Sometimes they make the first move against others to keep them off balance. They are like a boy who yells loudly to prove that he isn't afraid.

Insecure people often try to avoid getting hurt by others. They tend to be possessive of a tight circle of friends. Through this they hope to avoid being rejected or threatened. Often they surmise about why other people do what they do. Naturally, they judge other people to have the same negative attitudes they themselves have. Many times they are running when no one is chasing them.

What can you do if insecurity causes problems? The same thing, basically, that you would do for other emotional problems. First, bask in the security of God's love. Secondly, stop caring so much what others think. It's what God thinks that counts. Thirdly, don't try to protect yourself from every hurt. Live right, and accept whatever joys or sorrows that living right brings. In summary, forget about yourself and live for the Lord with all your heart. It will deliver you from a host of difficulties in your emotional life.

Living With Your Emotions

We've covered only a sampling of many areas in which a young man could have emotional struggles. Emotional problems are often related to spiritual problems. But they can be related to physical problems too, such as a chemical imbalance in the body, fatigue, or even a broken leg.

Sometimes you may need to receive help. From whom?

That would depend on the cause. Before you go to a doctor because your emotions are causing trouble, see whether you have a spiritual problem. Seek advice from a spiritual counselor. And don't take "spiritual" advice from someone who does not belong to the faith. Doctors have their place when the problem is physical, but can be damaging if trying to treat a spiritual problem. One such doctor told an acquaintance of mine that his church is too narrow and is the cause of his frustrations. That advice was not according to the Bible at all.

God is the only source of real healing and health. Trusting Him produces the only lasting peace and satisfaction. Walking close to Him day by day is the best source of strength there is. Then you can avoid the emotional pitfalls and enjoy the abundant life Jesus came to give. Take full advantage of it.

Chapter 12

Learning to Communicate

Mark threw himself wearily across his bed. He sighed deeply. "If only I knew what to do."

He lifted his head and listened. "It sounds as if they are still up. I know what I'll do."

Quietly he slipped down the stairs. His parents looked up in surprise.

"We thought you had gone to bed." Father laid his book aside. "Why don't you join us?"

Mark sank into the nearest chair. "Could we talk?"

"Of course," Father answered. "That's what we are here for. What's on your mind?"

Mark silently studied his fingernails for a moment. "I need your help," he said.

After an hour of discussion, Mark headed up the stairs with a lighter heart.

That looks so easy, doesn't it? But it isn't always. It can be very difficult to ask for help, even though we all need it at one time or another. To illustrate:

Lester looked out the window longingly. "If only I could talk to someone about my problem. But . . . the last time I tried, I couldn't express myself, and it seemed as if they just couldn't understand. Besides, ever since, they act rather strange. I'll just have to see my way through this alone."

Have you ever felt like Lester? I suspect that everybody has. Opening up to other people takes learning and practice.

But how important communication is! Communication links us to other people. It helps us to feel we belong. Without it, we are on our own and must find the answers to our problems ourselves. That leaves us unbalanced and vulnerable to our own weaknesses. We can be much stronger if we draw help from other people.

We communicate with words, mostly. But words and more words are not necessarily communication. Some people talk and talk but do not really communicate. Others are on the quiet side but communicate effectively.

Let me explain. Communication is more than transmitting information to others. It even goes beyond letting others know what we think or letting them know how we feel. Real communication is opening ourselves up and allowing others to see into our souls. Then too, communication is more than listening to people who open themselves to us. It means drawing near to them and trying to share their feelings.

Strangely, it seems that just when we need most to communicate, we find it the hardest. That's why, as a young man who wants to be strong, you need to believe in

The Importance of Communication

When you communicate by sharing your feelings, two things happen. First, saying how you feel can help you see yourself. I remember a time as a young boy when I was having a pity party for myself. My mother wanted to know what my problem was. I told her how terrible it was that I had not had the chance to go to town for a long, long time. Her question was, "What do you want there?"

You know, I couldn't think of a single reason. In a short time, I felt very sheepish because, by verbalizing my feelings, I saw myself.

This works for grown-up people too. Many times, sharing a problem helps us put it into perspective. Our own feelings and circumstances may have carried our thinking far afield. Saying what we think to others who have not had our experiences helps us see it through their eyes, even before they say a word. (Sometimes a wise friend repeats after us what we have just said to better help us hear it.)

The other value of sharing our feelings is that it gives others the opportunity to know where we are spiritually. That provides safety for us. Satan tries to destroy us by degrees, so having others monitor us gives protection.

There was a young man who never had much to say to his parents. He was quiet, easygoing, and pleasant, and showed good potential. Several years of his young manhood went by like this, and suddenly there was a tremendous breakdown in his spiritual life. He left the church and moved into an apartment in town with some of his newfound friends. What a shock! What had happened? He had slipped away gradually to a point that he himself admitted he had not expected. Had this young man been in up-to-date communication with someone, his slow decline may have been detected. Then someone could have helped him much more easily.

Young man, don't try to go through life on your own. You need the check of others on your life. Treasure their concern. It may be your lifeline.

Here a few other reasons why communication is important.

Communication helps us to learn. Sometimes we do not understand why we should believe Bible doctrines that we know people expect us to believe. Rather than harboring doubts, ask questions so that others can help you find answers.

Few people are balanced thinkers. Communication gives us the opportunity to try out our ideas and impressions on others. It works both ways. Sooner or later someone will ask you to listen so that he can try out his thinking on you.

Everybody needs advice. Communication is a good way to get it. True, some people think they know the answers without hearing the problem. But other people will hear you out. If you open up to them, they will have the opportunity to give you worthwhile advice. But if you don't communicate, then who can help you?

Did you ever wonder if anybody cares about you? Most people have flashes like that—their own private pity party. Everyone longs to feel important to someone and feels discouraged if he thinks he isn't. Most likely, people care about us more than we realize. But it takes communication with others to feel it—or to give them a chance to show it.

Sometimes people say they have no friends. It may be that they wear armor like a battleship and do not allow others to get close to them. Communication can help to dissolve their fears and encourage them to let their guard down.

We've been talking mostly about why *you* need communication. Remember, others need it too, from you. God wants you to communicate to let others know you care about them.

Risks in Communication

Communicating with other people is risky because it exposes our innermost being to them. We risk being misunderstood. Perhaps it is our fault: we may be too vague for them to understand. Or perhaps it is theirs: they may miss our point. They might catch some little thing we say and blow it up out of all proportion.

A man laid his heart bare to several other people about a spiritual struggle he was having. They reacted by saying, in effect, "Oh, we didn't realize that you were such a poor soul." He quickly retreated into silence. You can be sure he was far more cautious the next time—not necessarily to his advantage.

Sometimes we say one thing and others hear something else. You may say you don't like to get to church late, and someone may go away thinking you don't like to go to church! But being silent isn't the answer; that can raise questions too.

Sometimes we reach out to someone for help or support, and he fails to give it. It may be that we don't like to be too specific, and the other person does not know what we expect of him. But perhaps it is that the other person does not care enough to get involved. This hurts.

We may find that the other person is like a rosebush—looking good from a distance, but prickly when you get close. We may be disappointed in the character of another when it isn't as true as we thought.

Or we may catch a friend when he is mired in a difficulty of his own, too preoccupied to hear and to help us with our problems.

Are the risks too great? Of course not. But you must cope with them. What they should teach you is not, "Keep quiet," but rather, "Practice communication skills, and do it with the right people." Don't rob yourself of the blessings we have mentioned because you think crawling into a shell is safer.

Before You Can Communicate

Openness is a must before you can communicate. You can't be secretive and afraid of being known. How can you hide things and at the same time unburden yourself? How can you end with a light, clean feeling? It's impossible.

To communicate, you must be completely honest, not only with your words, but with the impressions you leave. It's all too easy to tell Joe you would like to spend Saturday afternoon with him and to tell Harry you are glad you don't have to. And both statements might be "true"—more or less—if you have mixed feelings on the matter. But the habit of telling everyone what you think he wants to hear can backfire when your friends start comparing notes. Besides, we might as well admit that it is not fair or honest. And without honesty, real communication is impossible, because people never know who the other person really is.

You must be ready to accept other people's input. If they sense that you let their advice go in one ear and out the other, don't be surprised if they have little time for you. Take their advice seriously—and appreciate it!

Be worthy of confidence. Others may share things with you that they do not want everyone to know. This shows that they trust you. They know that sometimes people share confidences only to find that others use the information against them. Do not betray another's confidence in you.

But what should you do if someone wants to tell you a secret, but you must first promise you won't tell anybody? And suppose it ends up being something that is wrong and needs to be exposed? That is one reason why it is wrong to promise to not tell anyone before you know what the secret is. You can promise to try to use wisely whatever others care to share with you. And if they do, treat it as a sacred trust.

Cultivate love. If love is not flowing, hearts do not open to each other. Unless the other person gets the feeling that you care about him, he will find it very hard to share with you. You must treat him in a way that he knows you consider him worthy of your time and affection. For you to show love is no more complicated than showing warm interest in the other person and concern for his well-being. Really, all we are to do is to show and share God's love.

You must also show respect for the person you hope to communicate with. You can do this by giving him your full attention. At the same time, don't be so intense that you make him feel uncomfortable. Don't be afraid to share a problem of your own—though that may make you feel small—and show that you can laugh at yourself. And don't pry. You can't open him up; he will have to open up himself.

Be ready to assume that the other person is sincere. Naturally, you will be disappointed sometimes. But if you distrust everybody, you can never communicate freely. Accept people at face value until they prove they are different from what they appear to be. Even then, believe that there is a spark in each person that your loving concern may be able to ignite.

Now for more practical talk on

Ways to Communicate

Remember that you always communicate more than your words say. Your tone, your face, and your body speak too. Recently a man stalked into a public shop where I was. Since I was the first person he met, he asked if I was the one taking up two parking spaces outside. While he spoke politely, something about his manner made me glad I wasn't!

Try first to confide in your parents. They probably know

your strengths and weaknesses better than you do. (There are exceptions to this rule, but not so many as young people tend to think.) You will need to be frank and honest. Tell them the whole story of why you need help. Be prepared to take their advice seriously.

Sometimes parents and youth find it awkward to discuss intimate problems. Maybe they have not shared enough in past days to be comfortable in freely opening up to each other. You must take time to share and visit with your parents to really know them. Don't get discouraged and give up if it seems hard at first. Do your part in starting conversations. I am sure you will find them very enjoyable.

Share some things with your spiritual leaders in the church. If you want to talk, say so. Don't expect them to catch a feeble hint that you would like to talk, because they might miss it. Be open and honest. Even though you may feel ashamed of having the problem, hiding it only compounds it. Neither can you receive the help you need.

In seeking answers, be sure to go to someone who will give you a frank diagnosis and not just smooth things over. We tend to talk to people who will tell us what we would like to hear, even if it isn't what we really need. (When you wanted to go fishing, did you ever go to the parent you thought would most likely say yes? Or, to whom would you go to ask advice about what type of car to buy?)

Look for evidence in these people's lives that they know how to make their advice work. You wouldn't think of asking your neighbor to fix your car engine if he has his own apart and doesn't know how to put it back together. A divorced person would make a poor marriage counselor. Recently a newspaper columnist who gave advice on personal matters to millions of people ended a thirty-six-year marriage in divorce. Should such a person be trusted?

Sometimes several people with the same problem try to help each other. While they might be able to give you sympathy and support, they might also help you feel too comfortable with a problem you ought to overcome. People sharing the same problem tend to justify each other rather than point to the real answer.

Beware of going to your own age group for help. With so few years of experience, your friends' perspective is too narrow to be dependable. Don't make the mistake Rehoboam made when he rejected the counsel of the sages and listened to those he grew up with.

Also, be wary of people with unsound spiritual or religious persuasions. They may reason away some very important Bible principles. That is why the Bible warns us to know whom we are learning from.

God, of course, is the source of all wisdom and direction. Don't neglect to seek Him. But remember that God often uses humans to help us find the way.

Cultivate small talk sometimes. Talking about the weather may seem trite to you. But it is a way of showing interest in people and being congenial. It is a way of getting onto the same wavelength. While talking to the Samaritan woman, Jesus demonstrated that one can lead the subject to spiritual things by starting out talking about natural things.

Take enough time to communicate. You may be in a hurry to get gas and be on your way, and yet the attendant may linger. The story he tells might seem boring. But if you expect him to listen to what you think is worthwhile, you need to hear him out. Don't be like those who have nothing to say unless the conversation is about them.

On the other hand, one can communicate too freely. This

can bring a snare. It is highly dangerous—even sinful—to become too intimate with those who are traveling the wrong direction spiritually. If you are an easy communicator, you need to be especially careful to stay aloof from the wrong type of people. Not that you shun them or act like you are so much better than they. But you must keep the line of separation between righteousness and unrighteousness clear. Many an easygoing young man has been drawn downward by not guarding his communications with the world closely enough. It's good to be congenial, but you may never do it at the expense of what is right.

Determine to be uncompromisingly good, no matter who you are with. Do not try to please everyone. Always seek what is best for others even if it is not what they are looking for.

Draw especially close to those who can help you on your way to heaven. Then you have support and encouragement available when you need it. You also have the security of knowing there are persons who can understand and help you if you falter. Being able to draw from their strength is a wonderful asset.

Communication is a gift from God. Don't waste it on earthly foolishness. If you use it God's way, you can have the benefits now and in eternity.

Chapter 13

Home Relationships

"The students at school think I'm lucky," said a young man with no home of his own. "I can come and go as I please." Then he added in a wistful tone, "But they have homes."

A good home makes a wonderful starting-off place for a young man. He has good habits and values riveted into him almost without knowing when it happened. If you have (or had) such a home, thank God. If not, determine that if you ever have a home, you will make it a strong home for God.

Your home, good or bad, cannot guarantee what you will be. Many a young man had a good home but never seemed to profit from it. After leaving home (or even before), he failed to appreciate the good things about his home. Years later, in many cases, he wished he could go back and start over. But he couldn't.

In the same way, praise God, many a young man has risen far above the home he grew up in. He embraced the right convictions and lived by them with little or no encouragement from his parents. It took strength to do that, but he became all the stronger because of it. The fact is, young man, that you yourself, and not your home, determines the kind of person you will be.

Right now is the time you must prepare to have a good home. The right way to start is to make the best of the home you live in now. Later we will discuss ways you can do this.

God established the home as the cornerstone of society. Here He intends for children to learn what real love is. Family members learn what it means to be part of a close-knit circle. They learn to get along with and help each other. This helps them learn how to be friendly and confident with people outside their family.

God wants homes to be stable and loyalties to be permanent. He put the marriage vows into granite by forbidding a man or a woman to forsake those vows and marry anyone else as long as each partner is living. He knew the home could never be stable with anything less than such permanence.

God also laid down responsibilities for each member. Naturally, we will talk most about the responsibilities of young men. The first responsibility concerns

Your Relationship to Your Parents

We discussed obeying and honoring your parents in an earlier chapter, so we will not rehearse that again. Here we are particularly interested in how you feel inwardly toward them.

First, you must have an *unconditional* love for your parents. You had that when you were young. You thought they could do everything. The way they did things was the right way. You loved them in spite of their mistakes.

By now you know they are not perfect. Perhaps they disappoint you at times. You might be tempted to think you will wait to love and respect them until they perform as you think they should. But that is conditional love. Unconditional love loves without waiting for sufficient reasons to love.

It is no doubt easier to love and respect your parents when you believe that they are sincere. But regardless of their attitude, they are still your parents. I can't explain how it all works, but when a young man refuses to accept his parents as they are, he loses more than a good relationship with them. His attitude affects his whole sense of values—even his attitude toward God. God planned that love and respect for parents be a necessary part of total character.

Have you ever wondered how several young people can grow up in the same home and take vastly different courses? Did the parents fail? Probably, because all parents fail. But is that the real and only reason? Do you know what I think makes the difference? It is what youth do with their parents' failures.

Let's face it. Most parents (perhaps I should have said *all* parents) make mistakes in raising their families. At least, they could have done better. But if children judge and despise their parents for their mistakes, they automatically take a giant step down the wrong road. The excuse that their parents influenced them wrongly is really no excuse at all.

As a parent, I am keenly conscious of the imperfections of my wife and myself. We pray that our children will love us so much that, in spite of our failures, they will embrace the values we tried to give them. I hope you will embrace every right value that your parents try to give to you.

Sometimes young people become resentful toward their parents because of their imperfections. You cannot afford to do this, because it will only make you bitter. You need to have a forgiving attitude toward them, or else you may end up even worse than they. Many a young man has.

106

Young man, don't forget that you owe much to your parents. They have put more into your life than you realize. No doubt they have made many sacrifices for you. They cared for you when you couldn't care for yourself. If you appreciate them for what they are, you will also be able to appreciate them for much they do. If you do this, you will be a real joy to them.

Sometimes young people feel their parents don't care much about them. Usually it's not that way at all. If your parents don't gush over you, that doesn't mean they do not care. Parents often assume that their children will sense how much they are loved without being told. If you are receptive to their love, you will likely feel it.

Don't take your parents for granted. Too often we wait until we don't have something before we realize how much it means to us. Stop and consider what it would be like without them.

Show your appreciation in little, everyday ways. Recently we were visiting in a home for several days. The teenage son thanked his mother a number of times for the good meal as he left the table. Sound reasonable? If you appreciate what your mother (or father) has done, say so.

Remember what appreciation is *not*. Some people think that appreciating parents means all kinds of gifts and extravagance. One mother always told her boys she would much rather have good boys than lots of gifts. The boys thought gifts would have been easier!

The best way to show that you appreciate your parents is to live uprightly. What could make your parents happier than that? What greater compliment could Ruth have given to Naomi than to say, "Thy people shall be my people, and thy God, my God"? Third John 4 says it for all serious parents:

"I have no greater joy than to hear that my children walk in truth."

Your parents are no doubt eager to have a close relationship with you. They like to know how you feel and what you are thinking. They are interested in what you do and where you go. You need to appreciate this interest. When you go away without them, tell them about it. Share your experiences with them. They are entitled to the enjoyable times you have. Let them be your best friends as well as your parents. It will be rewarding for both of you.

If you need help, let them give you advice. Even if they have no easy answers, you will certainly be encouraged by their concern. Many times encouragement is what we need most anyway, because, deep down, we already know what we ought to do. It might seem hard to approach them. (And then again, it might not; it doesn't seem hard for everyone.) At any rate, after the first few sentences, it probably won't be as hard as you may think.

God holds your parents responsible to give direction and to have order in the home. You need to respect their position and willingly fall into line with them. Don't waste time deciding how they should do things differently. That will only keep you from appreciating the good they do.

Taking instructions should come naturally for you. A bishop once asked a young son if it was hard for him to take instructions from his father. The young man said he had never even thought of that! It was a way of life for him.

We are speaking now of instructions you might not think of as important. What do you do when you are called to get up in the morning? What do you do if it's mealtime but you are reading a good book and aren't hungry? What if there is a sudden change of plans and you need to adjust yours to fit your parents'—can you do it graciously?

Perhaps you have the privilege of having brothers and sisters. We want to discuss

Your Relationship to Your Brothers and Sisters

If you are the oldest child, you might not realize how much the younger ones look up to you. Being the fourth child and the third son gives me a little insight into that. What older brothers and sisters do seems to be the way to do. Don't underestimate your influence over younger ones. Think of your place as a wonderful opportunity. You can help set the pace for the others who are following you.

Every child is important in a home—regardless of how many there are. Our children are still all at home. Whenever one of them is missing, there is a gap. When one is gone and we gather around the table at mealtime, someone says, "Where is everybody?" even though only one is missing.

Your brothers and sisters are there to be enjoyed. Don't miss having close ties with them. Sometimes older brothers think the younger ones are so very silly and childish. They may need to be reminded that they were that way too when they were younger.

While we are on that subject: you need to refrain from deciding what your parents should do when younger ones get out of hand. Leave that up to your parents unless for some reason it has become your responsibility.

Take pleasure in doing things together. Working together cements good friendships in the family. Younger brothers long remember the big brother who often says, "Want to come along?" or "Yes, you can drive it up the lane if you keep it in first gear," or "I'll let you paint the easy parts."

Even though we have touched many practical areas,

there are still many things you can do in

Contributing to Your Home Relationships

Don't forget that you have a large part in making your home a place you love to be. Sometimes young people get wrapped up in so many activities that their home is barely more than a motel and restaurant. Resist sliding into that habit. Make home the center of your life.

Busy yourself with projects and hobbies. Spend time reading and expanding your knowledge of worthwhile subjects. Learning to be content at home will be a real asset to you when you have a home of your own.

Home is also a good place to develop neat habits. Start in your bedroom. Try not to leave socks, papers, flashlight batteries, and key chains strewn here and there. Many a wife wishes her husband had learned more orderly habits when he was young!

Everybody in the house has rights. One of them is the right of ownership. Some things at your house are family property, and some are personal property. If a brother or sister has a tool or a book of his own, you have no right to treat it like family property. Everyone also has the right to some privacy. Don't barge into rooms that are not normal family living area. If a letter is not addressed to you or the whole family, you should get permission before reading it. It's not that these things are so highly secret; it's a matter of respect. You want the same for yourself, don't you?

Stand off to one side and act like a stranger. That's a sure way to make yourself feel like one. Be involved in family discussions. At family worship, be interested and take part. Even though you might not be the greatest singer, home is a place where that doesn't matter.

Enjoy being part of one of the best families in the world. After all, what family would you trade yours for? Once you realize what a good family you have, you will want to do all you can to keep it a good one.

Chapter 14

Church Relationships

Claude leaned against the church bench. "Yeah, I used to go to a church where people looked like this too. But I got tired of it."

Myron's eyes followed Claude's sweeping gesture. "Why? What do you mean?"

"Well, it's like this. I was raised east of here and used to go to a church close to home. And you know what? They just didn't seem to like anything I wanted to do. It was either my car or my clothes or the places I liked to go. Somebody was always on my back about something. So I left and . . . I just happened past today and thought I'd drop in."

"What are you doing now?" Myron asked.

Claude brushed his hair back from his eyes. "For a while I went south of us to a church there. But the same thing happened there. They expected me to do some things too. I just don't like . . ."

Myron moved to let several people pass by in the aisle. "Where are you going now?"

"I finally found something I like. Nobody tells me what to do. I do only what I have personal conviction for. And that," Claude emphasized, "is what I call real church. Don't you think you'd like that too?"

Myron hesitated. Before he could answer, Claude went on, "Don't you think a young fellow ought to be able to make up his own mind about some things without the church getting into it?"

"I don't know . . . about the church not being involved. I'm glad for the help I get from the church. Why—"

"But," Claude interrupted, "I wonder sometimes if the church is as important as some make it. Sure, I want to go to one, but . . ."

Sometimes other young men ask that question too. What part should the church have in the life of a young man like you? Does a young man need the church to be a strong Christian?

You know the answer to these questions, I am sure. Until the last few years, it was the accepted answer in practically every denomination. Lately, perhaps because many churches don't have enough life in them to make them attractive, some people say you don't need membership in any church any more—just worship wherever you please.

Let's test that idea. Whom did Jesus die for? Of course He died for sinners on an individual basis. But He didn't stop there. Acts 20:28 tells us that He purchased the church with His own blood. He redeemed sinners personally, but at the same time He redeemed them to bring them into a family relationship with God and His children.

The church is like the human family. I should say it is not only *like* a family, it *is* God's family on earth. God expects each one in His family to have a good relationship with the other children in His family.

Let me explain further. Let's think about

Why You Need the Church

To say it flatly, you need the church to survive. True, you may have heard of cases where believers had to live in isolation without contact with other believers. But those cases are rare indeed. Even in prisons, slave camps, and big, strange cities, God has a way of bringing believers together. That is to be expected, since God has deliberately designed believers to need each other. He could have made us self-sufficient and designed Christianity to be lived all alone. But He didn't.

You need the church in order to obey Bible teachings. You cannot possibly carry out all the Bible commandments by yourself. How could you be baptized or have Communion alone? Think also of all that the Epistles say about church life: "teaching and admonishing one another," "love as brethren, be pitiful, be courteous," "not forsaking the assembling of ourselves together," "bear ye one another's burdens." These are just a few.

You need the church to keep you balanced. The Bible says, "In the multitude of counsellors there is safety." Church leaders themselves need this. I have seen this happen when a group of ministers gathered to consider a problem. There would be a variety of opinions, but after a broad discussion, unity of thought developed. God uses other people to balance our thinking.

The church gives you a sense of security. Here you find acceptance and love. Here you find direction on the narrow road to heaven. And you also find correction when you need it. How different from insurances that help you if your house burns down—provided you have paid this month's premium. In the church, you don't need to worry that you haven't read the fine print. God's people help each other because they believe in bearing each others' burdens.

You see why God wants you to have a good relationship with the church. It is absolutely the only way to be a strong Christian. The idea that one can be on good terms with God and at the same time be on poor terms with God's people is wrong.

But does this mean that any group of people who call themselves a church is really a church? Since hundreds of groups call themselves churches, it can be very confusing. We must find out what God calls a true church. The Bible can answer the question,

What Is a Scriptural Church?

The Bible gives us several different pictures of the church. Ephesians 1:22 and 23 picture the church as the body of Christ, with Him as her head. Chapter 2 shows her as a building, with Christ as the chief cornerstone. Chapter 5 shows a marriage relationship, with Christ as the husband and the church as the wife. In all these illustrations, the church is a group of believers bound together by a spiritual relation with Christ.

A congregation is truly a church if Christ is her head, her cornerstone, and her husband. In other words, it is a true church if Jesus gives all its direction and inspiration. How does He do this? By speaking to the church through the Bible. So a Scriptural church is one that is following the Bible.

Still, that classification is so broad that most groups would probably claim that status. Can we discover a more exact definition of a true church? Yes! A true church requires all its members to obey sincerely all that the Bible commands, including those teachings which are not popular with the world. A true church travels the opposite direction from the world.

That should not be any surprise, should it? The church and the world are heading for opposite destinies. We cannot expect them to be traveling the same direction on the same road. No one can expect to live and act like the world and end up anywhere but where the world does.

An unscriptural church teaches only those Bible doctrines which are acceptable to the world. If antiwar feeling runs high in society, such a church gets out her peace banners. If society talks against racial discrimination, then in this church the preachers have a lot to say about loving people of other races.

A true church preaches peace whether loving your enemies is popular or not. Jesus taught us to suffer at other people's hands rather than to defend ourselves. In His church, nonresistance is law. That is why the Scriptural church cannot take part in war, government, law enforcement, lawsuits, and other forms of using force. The church has a heavenly calling and works in people's lives from the inside out, transforming them, not reforming them. (Government and law enforcement are good, of course, but they are not the responsibility of God's people today.)

A true church draws Biblical lines of conduct for her members. She has a perfect right (and responsibility) to do this; Christ expects the church to keep herself free from sin. She must also cut off the membership of those who resist the authority Christ has given her. Any other organization— a lodge or the armed forces, for example—sets rules and disciplines its members too. It is the only way for a group to function, or perhaps even to survive.

A true church demands nothing less than holiness. None of this: "I try to keep the Ten Commandments; I try to treat my neighbor right; I don't know much else, but I'm sure my minister could tell you." Beware of churches where members say, "Of course, I'm no saint. . . ." We had better be saints if we ever hope to see God.

By holiness we mean practical holiness. Many a preacher thunders against sin, but does not make applications. Or if he does, the congregation goes away saying, "I like a preacher that steps on my toes once in a while"—but they go on living as they always did.

Young man, the maze of many churches need not be confusing. Some young men have godly parents to guide them, and I hope you are one of them. Others are more on their own. Wherever you find yourself, seek God to lead you to a Scriptural group of believers. Perhaps, as other people have done, you can contact publishers whose literature teaches pure Bible doctrine. If you are truly sincere and ready to walk the narrow Bible way, God will lead you. He has said, "Ye shall seek me, and find me, when ye shall search for me with all your heart" (Jeremiah 29:13).

Look for a church group that is not living by the spirit and values of the world or seeking to please their fleshly and worldly desires. Rather, look for people with a humble, repentant, obedient spirit. Don't settle for a church that just talks about holiness. Make sure you can see it lived out in everyday life.

Granted, you will not find a perfect church. But here or there you will find a church where you can easily see people making a sincere effort to be all that God wants them to be. The evidence will show in every area of life: their values, their attitudes, their speech, their appearance. If the church's course is clearly Godward and not worldward, and her practices line up with Bible teachings, thank God for leading you to a right church.

That is enough about what the church ought to be. Now we will think about what *you* can do toward

Having Healthy Church Relationships

Sometimes it is said that young church members are the church of tomorrow. You are more than the church of tomorrow. You are the church of today, as much as any of the rest of us. True, you may not be in places of leadership. Yet you are exerting tremendous influence.

Do you know how much churches follow their young people? You know, of course, that the way young people embrace and practice the faith (or fail to embrace and practice it) will be just about what the church does twenty or thirty years later. But it is also true that young people influence their church while they are still young. Their dedication and quick (or slow) response to Christ's claims make a big difference in God's closeness to the whole group.

I have seen church leaders who were driven by unfaithful young people; they either allowed youth to have their own way or dropped them from membership. Instead of the youth making the necessary adjustments, the leaders gave in to the youth—thus the youth set the course. You never want to have part in influencing the church the wrong way, do you?

But real strength for the church—and for young men themselves—comes when young men team up with the church. Who needs a generation gap? No one is too young to support the church with all his strength. If you throw yourself into whatever contribution you can make, you will become stronger and stronger. The church will become stronger too.

Live up to what you promised when you became a church member. Nobody forced you to join the church; you volunteered. If you then drag your feet as a member, trying to get by with the substandard, you are not being fair to your commitment. Furthermore, you are not enjoying your membership. Neither are you fair to the people who took you seriously when you made your vows at baptism before God and all the people.

You need to know what you believe. Think through what the church stands for in order to develop convictions of your own. Don't be caught saying, "The church says so," when your neighbor asks you about your way of life. Be ready to give an answer from the Bible and from your own heart.

Take advice from others in the church. Look your brother in the eye when he gives it, and thank him, even if you are not sure you understand everything. Sometimes it takes awhile for us to realize how much we need help and direction. We tend to feel as confident and self-sufficient as Peter did when he boldly claimed he would never deny the Lord. Sometimes it seems that young men, especially, are tempted to be over-confident. It may be they haven't been around long enough to be disappointed in themselves as often as we older ones!

Be an active participant in the worship services. Choose a seat that shows you are involved—people don't choose the back rows for that. Sit up and be alert. Don't snuggle into a slouch—that makes your mind slouch too. Follow along in the Bible. Taking notes will help you to concentrate and to remember better.

Remember that the preacher sees his audience. It's a fact—your attention and expression can actually encourage or discourage him. Let the preacher know you want the straight truth—not only by telling him so, but better yet, by putting it into practice. That will help produce more good preaching.

Be involved in other church activities besides worship services. (A very latecomer to church saw the people coming out of the building and asked someone, "Is the service over?" The other man replied, "The service has just begun!") The church needs your help in distributing tracts, perhaps, or in visiting homes along with older members, or in mowing the cemetery or painting the spouting of the church building. Do it with your whole heart. Let me tell you, young man, nothing encourages older ones more than to see you take up the cross and follow Christ.

You will find all this to be pleasant, not irksome. If you chafe under good church life, take another look at your relationship to Jesus. That is the foundation for everything I have just said. I repeat, if we are on good terms with the Lord, we will be on good terms with the Lord's people.

Take it to heart, young man. God and the church need you, and yet not so much as you need God and the church.

Chapter 15

Purity Can Make You Strong

The world is wicked. Almost any direction you look, the billboards, the magazine racks, and even the people walking down the street display evil in front of you. You know this regardless of how sheltered you may have been. That the world is bad is no idle fact. The evil all around is setting snares for you personally. Many a young man has come to spiritual disaster when he was caught in the world's snares.

This danger did not take God by surprise. The Book of Proverbs gives a lot of attention to the matter of moral purity. Among all the snares spoken of in the book, impurity is given high priority.

Warning against a wrong relationship with an evil woman in Proverbs 7:26, 27, Solomon said, "For she hath cast down many wounded: yea, many strong men have been slain by her. Her house is the way to hell, going down to the chambers of death."

Young man, did you catch that? Strong men were among those brought down in defeat! Purity is an urgent matter for you. God has made it possible for you to be pure even in today's wicked world. But you must cooperate very closely with Him to do it.

Young men can sin in many more ways than the verse above mentioned. In this chapter we will talk much about what you think. Many bitter battles for purity take place in the mind.

Perhaps we should clarify a few terms. Moral life is an expression we often use. It means the proper (or improper) way a man behaves around women. It also means, especially for young men, one's control of his urge for sexual pleasure. Immorality, of course, is the opposite of good moral behavior. Chastity is another word for purity.

There are a number of strong reasons

Why Moral Purity Is Important

Being pure is the happiest way, or rather, the only happy way to live. Right here let's correct the false idea that God wants to hold people away from everything they like. Not at all. He never intended man to be miserable. Rather, He equipped us with instincts that when rightly used bring fulfillment. Every physical urge God gives us turns out to be wonderful when used in the right way. God planned that the natural attraction between men and women helps hold marriages together and make the lives of us all richer. It's the wrong use of what God created for good that He frowns upon.

Your moral life affects your spiritual life a great deal. It is true, a person might have high morals and still not be a Christian. But no one can live an immoral life and be a Christian. That is why Satan attacks a person in this area. If he can bring him down in his moral life, the spiritual life will follow.

Notice that the way you handle your physical instincts affects your life now—not just later. Moral impurity brings a troubled conscience. On the other hand, living a pure, victorious life in which you are the master of your body brings peace and a sense of God's blessing on you. Purity keeps the sky clear between you and God. What feels better than that? It is far more satisfying than a flash of impurity could ever be.

Purity will keep you from being destroyed. Look around you; do you see that immorality has the power to destroy? Look at all the broken homes. Think of the social diseases spreading by way of immorality. But worst of all, when a man deliberately commits moral sin, he loses his relationship with God. His spiritual life dies long before his home crumbles or his body gets sick.

You see, the threat is not only out there in the world. Satan also tries to destroy the most earnest Christians. Moral conviction can weaken from the inside if we do not guard it carefully. The process works a little like termites in the foundation of a building. The building does not collapse immediately. But if the termites are not stopped, sooner or later it will.

Two people I know come to my mind. Both of them were exposed to temptations in their work. Little by little they became careless about being upright and pure. After a number of months of weakening, they yielded entirely. Their lives were never the same again.

Sometimes temptation comes unbelievably fast. A young man can have a temptation thrust upon him totally unexpectedly. One young man was repairing a house, working alone. He was approached boldly by the woman of the house. Suddenly he found himself under severe test.

The danger lies not only outside us but also within. In your heart lives a traitor that always wants to open the door to Satan. That traitor is your own carnal nature. It constantly lusts after evil, and you must fear it.

You can hardly get too vivid a picture of the danger. The Bible asks, "Can a man take fire in his bosom, and his clothes not be burned?" The answer is clearly implied. "No!"

Since much of this has to do with you physically, we need to discuss

Understanding Your Physical Body

During your earliest childhood years, your body had two main drives—hunger and the desire for sleep. Now that you are maturing, another important drive is developing. This instinct is a natural part of God's plan to maintain the human race.

These developments are good in the right time and place, but your body does not know the right time and place. The reproductive organs begin to function long before a young man is man enough to handle parenthood. Controlling this drive before you get married will prepare you to control yourself more easily in later life.

Has God provided no way for the reproductive glands to find release? Yes, He has. From time to time, during sleep, the reproductive glands release their secretion from the body without any human assistance. Your body may seem to crave ways other than God's way. But your conscience knows better, and probably knew better even before you were told. The Bible implies in the second part of Romans 1 that even ungodly people have a fair idea of what is right and wrong. It also tells how utterly they each disgrace themselves if they do not listen to their conscience.

What you think affects your body. Your mind can stimulate your physical desires. Even more easily than you can think yourself thirsty, you can think yourself into wanting wrong things. Once the body is stimulated, it in turn stimulates the mind to think more wrong thoughts, creating a vicious cycle. God wants to deliver you from wrong thoughts when they first come to your mind, not two minutes later.

Remember, your old nature is never converted. Sin originates in our Adamic nature and then seeks to operate in our physical body. The body has no sanctified understanding of right and wrong. The old nature even prefers the unlawful over the lawful. The Bible says it seems to wicked people that "stolen waters are sweet, and bread eaten in secret is pleasant" (Proverbs 9:17). But note that the next verse tells us that such people end "in the depths of hell."

Much more could be said on the subject of your body. You need to be careful where you get your information. Authors, for example, who do not know God do not understand the sacredness of this part of life. Be sure to listen only to God's people.

Since the matter of purity is a weak spot for many young men, we need to learn more about how the devil lays many

Threats to Your Purity

One of the most threatening snares Satan lays is the indecency we see all around us. He knows that when women dress boldly and immodestly it tends to stimulate men's lusts. He knows that such scenes etch themselves deeply in the mind and are hard to escape.

Satan tries to enter through the ear-gate too. His people love immoral and filthy talk. They freely mention things too shameful to mention. Even if we hear their remarks and stories accidentally, they have a way of invading the mind and fastening themselves there. By ourselves, we cannot get rid of them.

Suggestive literature floods the market. Even supermarkets and drugstores display paperbacks, newspapers, and magazines with suggestive pictures and titles. It is hard to walk past them and not know they are there. You have probably felt the tug of the flesh for another look. Even the more "decent" magazines give a subtle, impure slant to their writing, because that is what society wants.

Television and radio spread sensuality very effectively. We are told that most popular songs describe or at least hint at immorality and illicit love. The descriptions are becoming more and more corrupt.

The invasion of VCRs (*V*ideo *C*assette *R*ecorders) has made corruption all the more available. Homes now become movie theaters. What people once watched in secret places they can now watch at home.

Sex perversion seems to be spreading. Homosexuality used to be called sin. (It still is sin.) Next, people began calling it a disease. Now they are pushing to accept homosexuality as normal! God will not tolerate these deviations from His wonderful purposes.

In some ways, judgment is already falling. For centuries already, social diseases have accompanied immorality. These diseases have defied prevention or cure. The AIDS epidemic is another example of the trouble man runs into when he is under God's disapproval.

You say you are a Christian and dead to the world's impurity? Good! But remember, even though your carnal nature can be crucified, it never dies to the point that it cannot rise again. It can still hear Satan's whispers. Unless you guard

126

against temptation and resist it, you will be sure to sin. Even the apostle Paul, victorious Christian that he was, said, "But I keep under my body [I keep my body under], and bring it into subjection: lest that by any means, when I have preached to others, I myself should be a castaway" (1 Corinthians 9:27). No wonder we all must be very serious about

Living a Pure Life

How wonderful that God gives power to live a pure life! Satan would like to make you think that when he tempts, you have no choice but to yield. That is not true. God has made a firm commitment to His children: "There hath no temptation taken you but such as is common to man: but God is faithful, who will not suffer you to be tempted above that ye are able; but will with the temptation also make a way to escape, that ye may be able to bear it" (1 Corinthians 10:13). Satan tries to wipe that promise away, but he cannot succeed.

When God lives in your heart and you give Him complete control, then you can be pure. He gives the power; your part is to surrender your carnal will and intensely desire to please Him.

Of course, the victory is not easy. Satan never gives up. Neither does the old carnal nature. You will need to fight a hand-to-hand battle with them both. You will never conquer them once and for all. The battle will be constant—many times a moment-by-moment struggle. But the good news is that you can find a moment-by-moment victory.

Settle the heart of the matter first. Who owns your body? Is it yours to do with as you please? No, God owns your body. His wishes for your body must be honored. First

Corinthians 6:13 says, "Now the body [your body] is not for fornication, but for the Lord; and the Lord for the body."

Did you notice that the principle works both ways? First, you must not sin against the Lord with the body because He owns the body. Better yet, if the Lord is *for* the body, He can give the power for victory, can He not?

Should you ever fail in your personal life, don't give up. Go back to God in repentance and with a determination to be closer to Him so it doesn't happen again. Stay committed! Then you can count on His forgiveness and help in the future. Never allow Satan to get you to think there is no point in trying to stay pure.

Guard your mind closely. Proverbs 4:23 says, "Keep thy heart [mind] with all diligence; for out of it are the issues of life." It is in the mind that you entertain or refuse temptation.

Have the right goals. We think about how to be what we want to be. The person who wants to be rich thinks about how to get rich. Staying strong and pure for God must be at the top of your list of goals.

Learn to say no to evil thoughts and stick to it. Did you ever half entertain a thought and half fight it at the same time? As a rule, what you do not entertain, you will not have to fight. Say, "Get thee behind me, Satan!" and ask God to give you something else to do or think about.

You must also be able to say no to people who would tempt you to sin with them. Sometimes you must promptly walk away. Whatever it takes to stay pure, do it. The way you act will tell others whether you are interested in sin or not.

The most important practical thing you can do is this: *keep your mind busy with good things.* You cannot possibly keep temptation out of an empty mind. "Idleness is the devil's workshop" never fits anywhere better than right here. A mind busy with good things can resist evil much more effectively when it comes knocking. Memorizing Scripture is one of the best ways of filling and occupying the mind.

The way you use your spare time affects you. Be involved in a hobby or a craft or something useful. You will find that it stimulates self-respect. And, very important, it helps to keep your mind occupied. Keep something like this handy, and when temptation comes, get busy at it.

Some people have one weak spot; other people have another. Know what you find most tempting for yourself. If temptation comes strongest to you at bedtime, be sure not to spend time idly in bed. Read your Bible or some good book until you are sleepy. Or get out and do something else. Avoid situations that bring physical sensations that make purity more difficult. If you have a weakness for the impure magazine covers on newsstands, you may need to stay out of certain stores. There are many places a Christian has no business being. Sometimes the "way to escape" that God has promised is to never get close.

Refuse to think about the evil you couldn't help seeing. Don't even meditate on the shockingness of it; just dismiss it. Many a young man thought he could get away with indulging in wrong thoughts only to fall into what he had fantasized. Remember that the evil you absorb in your mind is difficult to get rid of. Someone lamented over how hard it was to forget what he wanted to forget and how hard it was to remember what he wanted to remember. That applies here very well.

Your friends affect you very much. Someone has said, "Tell me what your friends are like, and I know what you are like." If they make it harder for you to live a pure life, are they really your friends? Really, they are your enemies.

Choose friends who inspire you to be strong. And be sure to be the same kind of friend to them. Then you can help each other stay pure.

Consider the environment in which you work. It is far better to work for a lot less money in a good environment than to risk your purity in a bad place for more money. See if you can work with someone who shares your desire to be pure so that you can be each other's keepers.

Finally (although more could be said), stay close to spiritual people. In the matter of morals, it is very valuable to share with someone who understands your struggles and can help you. Don't be ashamed to expose your battle. All of us men have our struggles to be pure—older ones too, from time to time. It is the men who *don't* struggle that disappoint us.

Staying pure, after all, is not the negative subject some people make it out to be. Yes, there are some "Thou shalt not's." We speak of mortifying the flesh and crucifying the old man. But don't forget that when the old man is crucified, the new man can live. As the apostle Paul said in Galatians 2:20, "I [the old Paul] am crucified with Christ: nevertheless I [the new Paul] live; yet not I, but Christ liveth in me . . ." Paul lived a pure life and received the great honor of Christ living within him. So can you. God wants you to be glad to be pure. He needs men like you so much in today's sad world.

Chapter 16

What You Read

What would your world be like if you could not read? Your first thought might be, "It would be hard to find a job." True, but reading makes you rich in ways that have nothing to do with earning money. If you could do the experiment of going one day without being able to read, you would probably be astonished at how often you would miss reading. You would be like a newly blind man who says, "I never knew before I became blind how much I use my eyes!"

I know numerous people who cannot read. I have seen them at the bank or applying for a driver's license. Although they can get along all right in conversation and in common-sense situations, they must cope with terrific disadvantages. Most of us are greatly blessed by the fact that reading comes naturally for us. It has been a part of our world ever since we can remember. Probably nothing has expanded our minds more than reading and being read to.

Reading has molded the civilized world. And what we read will mold us, whether we like it or not. Even our casual thoughts as we wash the car or walk down the street have much to do with what we have been reading.

God knows the value of reading. He wrote on the tables of stone for Israel. He had the prophets write, and write again. He directed the apostles to write letters to the churches. Finally He had it all preserved in a book, the Bible. Reading unlocks its treasures for us.

In another chapter, we will deal more thoroughly with reading the Bible. In this chapter, we will discuss reading in general. We want to consider further why

Reading Is Powerful

When giving job interviews, some companies ask the prospective employee what book he read last. Or, better yet, they ask what book he is reading now. Why? They claim it tells them a good bit about his values and tastes. It also tells them much about the size of his mind.

Nothing sharpens the mind like reading. It's a much more active process than watching television. Reading takes thinking. It is an effective way to store things in your mind so that they stay there. Did you ever make a store list, read it, and not need it again? I have. Writing and reading give the mind exercise and help it to recall information. Even when the mind has a vast accumulation of knowledge, it takes reading to keep the mind sharp.

Books can be your good friends. They can take you places your feet will never go. They can make you think deep and hard. They can teach you things no friend has thought to tell you. They can kindle your aspiration and help you establish goals. Many a man can point to a certain book that profoundly influenced his course in life.

However, books can influence you for bad as well as for good. Just to show you how it can work, consider this: Charles Darwin proposed the theory of evolution in his book

The Origin of Species. He died without seeing his ideas bear fruit. But his message remained and was later used by avid readers as a basis for the erroneous idea of evolution. Who hasn't heard of evolution today? The same could be said of Karl Marx's *Das Kapital.* He died without seeing what socialism would do (and fail to do) for Russia today. Yet socialism continues, largely because of the seed he planted when he wrote that book.

Thank God, the same process works when men write the truth. Many people have been blessed by Daniel Kauffman's *Doctrines of the Bible* (for just one illustration), even though he has long gone to his reward.

Young man, you will not want to neglect the opportunity to become strong through reading. It can help equip you to be useful to God. Since reading becomes part of us, and powerfully influences us, we must consider the

Dangers in Reading

Anything powerful is dangerous. A loaded gun, a powerful motor, ten thousand dollars—all are dangerous if not handled carefully. Reading is like that.

Some people read so much that they hardly have time to live. One of my classmates in school was such a reader. The teacher could hardly get him outdoors at recess. At home, about all he did was read. But he was not a practical person. Changing a flat tire or fixing the back porch would have been very difficult for him because he didn't live in a real world.

Some people actually prefer to live in a world of fantasy and imagination. To them, reading is an escape. Now it is true that reading should be a journey of the imagination. As we read, we travel with the character we are reading about. We sigh or smile with him. We hold our breath and hurry to the next chapter. That naturally goes with reading a good story. It is a problem only if we hate to come back to reality.

Too much light reading is damaging. Usually, reading in the form of stories draws you into the action and makes it harder for you to stop than to keep on. Much light reading creates a lazy mind that thinks, "I want some excitement when I read. If reading requires concentration, no thanks. That's too hard and dry." If this kind of reader comes across writing that forces him to come to conclusions by careful reading and deduction, he simply lays it aside. How about yourself; do you read the adult church periodicals? Or do you have interest only in story-type material?

Beware of writing that reasons and philosophizes, but does not give you any real direction for living. When reading leaves you satisfied to only think and talk rather than to act, something is wrong. Philosophy books have destroyed many people by leading them to reasoning rather than to simply obeying Bible truth.

Do not trust your favorite authors too much. If we like what someone writes, we tend to become gullible. Just because he speaks soundly on certain issues doesn't mean he is safe in all other areas. Sometimes it is what a person does not say that makes him dangerous. Some of my acquaintances liked one popular writer so much they let their guards down. One of them said in discussing a particular issue, "I don't know his position on that issue, but I'm sure he's right!" But the Bible tells us, ". . . knowing of whom thou hast learned them" (2 Timothy 3:14).

Then there is also the danger of not reading enough. A young man just out of school may feel he has done enough reading for a while. Maybe his work doesn't demand much reading. Or perhaps he thinks he is too busy. Usually, several years later, he wishes he had not left off reading. His mind has not been stimulated lately. Reading is to the mind what food is to the body. Without input, there will not be very much useful output.

Good reading habits will help you avoid many of these dangers. But these habits don't come walking to you. The fact is,

Reading Requires Discipline

You can't get by with eating only food you like. Can you imagine what you would be like by now if you had had all the dessert and candy you wanted as a boy? So it is with reading. Just liking to read isn't the answer; you have to like to read the right things.

At your age, you would probably say, "I like a few sweets but mostly solid food." How did your tastes change? You simply ate certain foods regularly until you liked them. We nearly always learn to like what we live with. When foreigners come to America, they prefer their old home foods over what we may prefer. Some friends of ours moved to the Philippines when their children were small. Now their children prefer rice over potatoes. That preference will likely change now that they are back in America.

Our reading appetites are like that. Some types of reading are like candy—a little is all right, but too much would be damaging. The newspaper and news magazines could be put in that category. Also included here are the industrial trade and farm magazines. They can be intoxicating.

Everybody likes to read stories. They are relaxing and interesting. But a story that just begs for another story gets to be meager fare. There isn't enough substance to it, because it answers its own questions and doesn't need any response from you. How far would you get at your job if you worked only at what is easy, relaxing, and enjoyable?

Watch your casual reading. Most printed matter today is geared to attract the casual reader. (Watch what people do in waiting rooms—be it at the doctor's office or in the airport.) Even at home, I know how easy it is to pick up whatever is handy and bury myself in it. The question is, is it really the most important thing I could be reading right now? Keep a good book by your bed, on your desk, or in your suitcase when traveling. You will find moments you can capture and put to good use if you are alert to them. They are golden moments.

It is also good to block out a specific time of the day to read. Someone has said that fifteen minutes a day will get you through any book.

To read weighty, concentrated material, you must take your mind firmly in hand. Although you may feel like leaning back in your chair and floating along, discipline yourself to read deeper than that. Taking notes or underlining key thoughts will help you understand and remember the facts better.

What if you just don't enjoy reading? Is there any hope? Yes, there is if you are persistent. You can learn to enjoy reading. If your vocabulary is poor, keep a dictionary handy, and you'll be amazed how quickly you'll learn the regularly used words. Most people who learn to read well later in life started with easy material. One father who had very little schooling started by reading his children's Sunday school papers.

The discipline of reading will reward you well with enjoyment. It will also help to develop you. That is why we must yet discuss

What Shall I Read?

Remember that what we like to read is determined largely by what we want to be. So you must have high goals for yourself. You must determine to read what is going to help make you stronger spiritually. What should it be?

Of course, the Bible needs to come first. In fact, much of what you need to read is various forms of Bible teaching. That puts the church periodicals next on the list. Some of this material may not seem as exciting as you think it should be. But you still need it.

Just a hint: if you feel it should be better, why not try writing? This is not a rebuke, but a challenge. The Lord is always looking for good writers. Writing is a craft for people who are ready to work hard at doing better. One writer said it's not that he's a better writer than others—he just tries harder!

At any rate, you need to have a special appreciation for your church publications. They represent the beliefs you have chosen to identify with. Reading them will help you stay abreast with the thinking of the church and her leaders.

As a young man, don't read only the youth-level papers. Graduate into the adult material as well. You like to do grown-up things, don't you? This will help you to become strong.

Open your eyes to the many good Bible study books available. Authors who are sound in doctrine have much to offer. Many of them have put much research into a small package. One such writer is said to have read a book in the Old Testament close to eighty times before he wrote anything about it. Reading the work of such men gives us the benefit of their work.

Some books give you side truths that make the Bible clearer. For example, a book about manners and customs in Bible times can help you understand certain sayings and actions in the Bible. (Did you know that "treading the winepress" is literally what people did in Bible times? They tramped on the grapes in the winepress to squeeze out the juice.) Some of these books are heavy reading and require discipline. Do not let that stop you; think of them as a challenge.

Many storybooks are on the market. Some are enjoyable and helpful. But remember, read only those that hold up high standards of purity and Christian conduct. The market is flooded with mixtures of religion and sensuality. Books involving romance are written for the sensual part of you, not the spiritual, even if they contain some religion. They will not help prepare you for Christian love and marriage; in fact, they will give you unrealistic ideas about what to expect. Books such as these make it harder for a person to adjust to real marriage. It is unwise for a single person to spend a lot of time reading about married life—especially the way such books portray it. Such a habit will also keep you from enjoying the present the way God wants you to.

Books about nature are interesting. They broaden one's awareness and understanding. Jesus had a wealth of wisdom about life and nature which He used freely in illustrations. I enjoy exploring the world about me by way of books and seeing it through the eyes of others.

Biographies are often good reading. They help us see how others faced life—the same kind of life we face. Many individuals I have lived with in books have influenced my life. The ones who lived for an unselfish cause higher than their own personal interests are especially meaningful to me. Biographies of spiritual church leaders of the past are especially valuable. Of course, you must beware of swallowing the hidden biases of authors, who have a way of writing only about those facts they want you to know.

Then there is history. Who of us has not wished he knew more about it? Religious history is of special interest to most Christians. They want to be well versed in the issues men have lived and died for. The *Martyrs Mirror* is one of the most powerful books ever printed. It tells why and how believers triumphed over disgrace, drowning, burning, and long, long imprisonments. I am encouraged every time I read about their faithfulness even to death. History also holds accounts of failure and defeat. We need to learn from them too.

Devotional books can be valuable too. They can help you develop a deeper personal worship of God. You don't want to depend solely on the ideas of others. But they can be a pump primer for you. (To prime the hand pump in the old days, you had to pour a little water in it to get it going.) Devotional books give you a few ideas to get your own ideas started.

Strictly secular books can give you valuable information on anything from welding to hummingbirds. But you need to guard against merely wanting knowledge to feed your ego.

What about newspapers and news magazines? Read with care. It is possible to become addicted to news. Consider also the increasing explicitness (shall we say brazenness?) with which newsmen describe wickedness. It's debatable how much of that kind of reading we can handle without starting to meditate on it or even contemplate practicing it. Someone advised, "Always read the newspaper standing up." Certainly we must not allow it to become the major part of our reading diet.

Young man, your mind is like a sponge; it soaks up

whatever you give it. Determine to read only what will help you face life properly and make you useful to God. Give your mind only what is worthwhile. Then your reading can help make you strong.

Chapter 17

Your Devotional Life

Dean waited patiently until most of the people had left the church building. "Brother Samuel, do you have a few minutes to talk?" he asked.

"Of course. I'll meet you in the basement in a few minutes." Brother Samuel smiled. Later in the basement, he asked, "Young man, what's on your heart? I noticed you looked perplexed during the message."

Dean looked off into the distance. "Your sermon on devotional life really stirred me. I know that what you said is true, and I have experienced it, but . . . it isn't always like that. It can be so hard . . ."

"Son, what is it like when it is going well?"

"Why, God seems so close to me and I find it so much easier to deal with temptation. Everything goes so much better," Dean answered.

"And how is it when it isn't going well?" the minister probed.

"That's just it. There are times when the Bible doesn't seem to come alive and praying seems almost as if I'm talking to myself. And then, of course, I am not as strong as I need to be," Dean confided.

"And what are you looking for?" Brother Samuel asked, leaning toward him.

"I want the kind of devotional life that helps me feel close to God and provides that daily strength to live for Him. I want to be a strong young man," Dean stated with conviction.

"God bless you, Brother. You are on the right track." Samuel smiled. "I want to give you all the help and encouragement I can."

Do you understand Dean's feeling? Every serious believer wants that close touch with God. It is the only way to have power in our spiritual lives.

An effective devotional life does not just happen. Dean knew it. Brother Samuel knew it. And we do too. So let's explore it together.

The devotional life is a pivot point in the Christian's life. The strength he has in his spiritual life is the result of being in touch with God. Wherever there is power over evil and inspiration to do right, it comes from God.

The reverse is also true. When the believer is defeated and not recovering, you can be sure that his devotional life is not what it ought to be. A believer's devotional life is his fountain of spiritual strength. If that fountain runs dry, there is trouble ahead.

The term "devotional life" means different things to different people. What does it mean to you? What does it leave you looking for? I'll try to explain

What Devotional Life Ought to Be

Devotional life is not a group activity; it is between you and God. A similar term is "personal worship." We will use both terms along the way, depending on what aspect we are emphasizing.

Personal worship is more than just reading a chapter and saying a little telegram-like prayer to God. Some people try to worship the same way they drop in on a McDonald's fast-food restaurant—rushing up to the counter, ordering a bite to eat, and hurrying on their way. They think this bit of time for God is a quick fill and a quick fix for the day—only to wonder later what went wrong.

To worship is to deepen a friendship—between a child and his father. You approach God with respect and awe, and yet with confidence. You know that your Father is pleased to have you come to Him. The Bible says, "Draw nigh to God, and He will draw nigh to you" (James 4:8). You and God share with each other, sometimes actively, sometimes quietly.

A father was trying to analyze what fellowship with God really meant. His child climbed up and disturbed him. Wishing to get rid of him, the father asked the child what he wanted. The child's reply: "Oh, nothing. I just wanted to be close to you." There was the father's answer about fellowship with God!

It is impossible to draw close to God and remain the same person. Did you know that we become like what we worship? According to Psalm 135:18, even idol worshipers are like their idols. Second Corinthians 3:18 shows us how it works in us Christians: "But we all, with open face beholding as in a glass the glory of the Lord, are changed into the same image from glory to glory, even as by the Spirit of the Lord."

In the end, the time for personal devotions is only a high point in a whole life of devotion. No one can really worship God without totally giving himself to Him.

An army company demonstrated this principle. The

soldiers almost worshiped their captain. If he asked for ten volunteers for a dangerous mission, there was a rush to be first. In spite of the fact that it meant almost certain death, they were ready. That was personal devotion. And that is what God wants from us.

Worship is a spiritual exercise, so it may be difficult to measure its quality. But then, you have never seen the wind either—but you can feel it and see the results. Even though personal worship takes place in the heart alone before God, you can know it happened. Let's discuss a few results that show

What Devotional Life Can Do For You

Some people are contagious. Their zest for life rubs off on you. You can't help but be inspired by their spirit. One daughter told me, "When Daddy comes home from a visit with his friend George, he has 'that gleam' in his eye." I like being around that kind of person too. But God can inspire people better than any man can. Remember what being on Mt. Sinai with God did for Moses?

In personal worship, we give God the chance to reassure us that He is there. When the "God is dead" idea was going around, one bumper sticker countered with, "God isn't dead. I talked to Him this morning."

Worship reassures us that God is interested in our particular needs. It gives us a calm outlook on our day because we know that God will be "out there." We can face problems and decisions with confidence and courage.

Worship also helps us to put life into perspective. As a song says, "Our vision fails, our sense of life's proportion, unless we seek the quiet place of prayer." The rush of life crowds out the eternal aspects of life if we don't take time to worship. The psalmist experienced this. He said, "My feet . . . had well nigh slipped . . . until I went into the sanctuary [presence] of God; then understood I . . ." That job, that investment, that shattered dream will lose its grip on you when you measure it against eternity.

Once we realize that God is guiding our day, we need not fear temptation. It can actually help us to grow. Stumbling blocks can be turned into stepping stones. Life becomes an adventure of finding out what God has planned for us today.

It all adds up to rest for the soul. When your soul rests in God, you are strong. Does that sound too easy? It is possible—realistically possible. However, you must overcome the

Problems You May Face

The devil strikes hard at our devotional life because it is the supply line between us and God. He knows that if we stop communicating with God, we are finished. So he does all he can to frustrate and destroy our regular contact with God. Let's be prepared to face the problems he causes.

First, consider the problem of lack of urgency. How important do you think it is for you to have a daily encounter with God? What difference does it make in your day? Unless you see it as a vital link to God, you will lose the sense of urgency about a regular personal worship.

Next, we want to discuss the problem of a lack of love for God. Really, this is probably a major root of problems in devotional life. Lack of love for God makes people lose their desire to fellowship with God. Their eagerness to obey disappears, and when they do obey, it is out of a sense of duty rather than love. Devotional life then becomes a drudgery.

When love is gone, what is left?

Love for God does not vanish overnight. It disappears bit by bit. Simple neglect may be its worst enemy. If not fed, love dies slowly but surely. You can easily neglect your devotional life because of failing to plan properly for it. You can allow small interferences to keep you from getting it done. You may be "too tired" when it's time. Or you might get up too late. Whatever the excuse, neglect threatens us all.

Another problem is time. How and when can a busy person manage to spend time with God regularly? Daily duties call us from the moment we wake up. If we plan to have our time with God later, we usually find that all day other things keep us occupied. Finally evening comes. Does time come easily then? Not always. But the problem of time must be solved, or there will soon be worse problems.

As you well know, sin, or any kind of rebellion toward God, spoils the desire for personal worship. Guilty people avoid God. They do not pray or read the Bible much, because this reminds them of their marred relationship with God. Their only cure is repentance.

One more practical problem is the lack of immediate results. Sometimes our devotional activities may seem dull. We sense no excitement or fine warm feeling. This is actually normal at times, a way and time that God wants us to exercise faith and prove our steadfast love to Him by continuing on with Him. But if we don't realize that God is watching to see how we face the test, we can develop a "what's the use" attitude.

Lack of concentration in Bible reading and emptiness in prayer are also potential problems. Any of these, or a combination of them, are a deadly force. They can happen to you—and quickly—if they are not guarded against.

146

No doubt there are other problems besides these. But these suffice to show that the battle is real. We must handle them in an aggressive way. Although there is no quick, easy remedy, we can do some things to avoid many of these problems. Here are some suggestions for

Getting What You Need

The ideas that follow will not do the worshiping for you. You could go through many such motions and still not worship. Think of these suggestions, not as magic cures, but as avenues to lead you to the Lord. Consider them prayerfully.

First, you need to meet God on a daily basis. You must have a particular time of the day when you do this. The time needs to be a combination of what fits your schedule and what best meets your needs. Personally, I think every child of God needs to take time to meet Him in the morning. It is better to be equipped to face the day and then not need to mend so much at night. If it does not fit in the morning, try a better time. But stick to that time. Do not just try to have your time with God whenever it fits in. You know the end of that—and it will be an end, all right. It's good to spend some time with God before retiring at night regardless of when you have your main devotional time with the Lord.

Through the Bible, God speaks to us as if He had written a letter. But the Word of God is much more than that! The Holy Spirit works through the Bible, causing it to come alive. It becomes food for your soul.

But you must digest it and absorb it into your system. Read the Bible carefully, thoughtfully, and prayerfully. Come to it like a bee that sticks its tongue deep into each blossom. Don't be like a butterfly that just flits from one place to the other. Read it slowly, word by word or phrase by phrase. Sometimes read it rapidly to get a bird's eye view. Let God impress you with the truth He has for you today.

Keeping a notebook where you can write promises and impressive thoughts can be valuable. Write what you intend to do with the message of truth. Check on yourself later. Whether you cover verses or chapters, be sure you uncover a thought to take with you.

Devotional guidebooks may have a place. But don't let them keep you from getting into the Bible. Make sure they lead you into the Bible rather than becoming an end in themselves.

Keep in mind that your main purpose in personal worship is to gain food for your soul. You can make in-depth studies of the Bible and study your Sunday school lesson at other times.

Regarding prayer, what is it? The simplest definition is talking to God. We need to do lots of it. Even before you read the Bible, you should ask God to direct you in your reading. Try to get away from the idea that God talks to you for a certain time through the Bible and then you talk to Him for a time in prayer. You would have a hard time visiting with a friend like that. Prayer should be a fellowship in that you and God communicate back and forth.

How? When you wait before God during prayer, you give Him the opportunity to communicate with you through the Spirit. He can direct your mind and conscience to think after Him. Have you ever prayed about a problem you were facing and then thought of the answer to what you prayed for? That is God at work! This waiting is not something like letting our minds just go blank. It's more like thinking aloud to God.

Prayer time is not the time to instruct God. Neither is it like talking to a store clerk we expect to be our servant.

It is not just to present a long list of please do's, please give's, and please bless's. We need to be careful not to be bossy and insistent. God may have something better for us than what we are asking for. Besides, what God has to say to us is more important than what we have to say to Him.

Be yourself in prayer. Don't just rattle off a half-memorized prayer. If you use a prayer list at times, don't always pray about the items in the same order. Think about what you pray, and mean what you say.

Sometimes we tend to talk to God about others and not about ourselves. But don't be afraid to tell God how you feel. Telling God if you feel discouraged or frustrated can be a big step toward healing. Honestly confess your wrongs too. There is no point in wearing a mask—God knows what is behind it. And He knows what it takes to get us back on track!

Don't forget to be thankful. The problems you prayed about yesterday didn't just happen to work out all right by themselves. Give Him the honor for that.

Real prayer includes praise—something different, and in a way, higher than thanksgiving. Praise is appreciating God for what He is and not only for what He has done. Casual thankfulness without praise stops when the blessings seem to have stopped. Thankful praise never stops! Habakkuk will tell you about it in chapter three, verses seventeen and eighteen. Don't hesitate to ask God for things. He invites, yes, commands us to ask, even though He already knows our needs. He wants us to admit that we are helpless and are depending on Him. He is eager to help if what we ask is unselfish.

Think of God as a friend. You know, the Bible says that Abraham was "the friend of God." In other words, God has people for His friends. That tells me that we have a friendly

God! All we have to do when He knocks is to open the door, and He will come in and sup with us, and we with Him.

Young man, personal worship is a rewarding experience. Apply yourself to these practical suggestions, being careful to do it in a true spirit of worship.

Finally, remember that true worship is a total way of life. The question is not so much, "How are your devotions?" as it is, "How is your *devotion?*" God wants to walk with you all day long—not only during a time of worship. Then He can be to you what you need to be—a strong young man.

Chapter 18

Music and You

Music is a powerful force. God has a good purpose for it. But Satan also uses it very skillfully to his advantage.

A musician estimated the power of music something like this: "If you let us write the nation's music, we don't care who writes the laws. We will be in control."

That is no empty statement. The invasion of drugs and immorality first stimulated by rock-and-roll music proves this truth. People's behavior at rock concerts demonstrates its intoxicating power.

On the other hand, songs of praise, aspiration, and consecration have always given a real spiritual lift to believers. The rhythm and tunes help to make the words easy to remember—even subconsciously.

I think you recognize the dangers of worldly music. You know that a Christian can not soak up that kind of music and not be deeply affected by it. Yet even a young man who is converted and realizes this finds that his old carnal nature is not too dead to prick up its ears when he hears the wrong kind of music. That is why we need to discuss it.

In a sense, the man makes his music and the music

makes the man. Someone has said, "Know the music a man likes, and you can pretty well guess what kind of car he drives, what kind of clothes he wears, and what his haircut looks like." So any young man who wants to be strong spiritually must control his musical tastes.

The influences of music are often subtle. It is hard to recognize them for what they are. Hopefully, our discussion here will help give you a sharper ear so you can separate the good music from the less good. It should also sharpen your conscience to help you know which music to enjoy and which you must reject. Then you can discover God's real purposes for music.

For the sake of clarity, I should mention that people often associate the term *music* totally with musical instruments. But the word also includes singing, and we will use it that way also.

First, you must understand

How Music Reaches You

Man is a three-fold being—body, soul, and spirit. Music affects all three.

The body easily senses rhythm. As you walk beside a friend, sometimes you subconsciously fall into step with him. It is easy to respond to music in the same way, especially if you are musically inclined. Standing in line at an airport recently, I saw a man twisting and swaying as if he were in terrible pain. His eyes were glazed, and he had a faraway look. Then I saw he was wearing earphones. Quite apparently he was listening to some kind of music.

Satan has exploited bodily response to music for a long time. Dancing and the beat of the music that goes with it stimulate sensations in the body that generate passion and other wrong desires.

Obviously, the soul too is affected by bodily stimulation. The soul is the real you. Your soul makes your choices and determines your values. In the soul, affection grows.

Wrong music affects your soul through the body, partly by the beat and partly by the words. Whether you hear the words clearly or whether they are half lost in the music, they stir unholy thoughts. The suggestions of illicit so-called love, passion, and other forms of wickedness make an impression on the soul. While the mind may barely be aware of what it is hearing, the ideas are penetrating the mind just the same. Have you ever had words come floating through your mind from a song you hardly knew you had heard?

The spirit is the third part of us. Because of Adam and Eve's Fall, we all start out dead to God in spirit. But our spirits can be regenerated again through the new birth and become alive to Jesus Christ. The music we feed on helps to determine the health of our spirit.

Unregenerated people care mostly about their bodily sensations. They have no desire to please God. But a spiritual man is different. He wants what he feasts on to feed his spirit. He fears any influence that would lead him away from God.

Since music has such a powerful effect on us, you must recognize

How Music Can Weaken You

A flat tire is never "just flat on the bottom"—it is simply flat. If you weaken in music, you are simply weak. Weakening toward sensual music will make you a sensual person. Weakening toward any kind of wrong music will give you a weak conscience. It will drown out the painful cry of an empty soul. King Saul was using music to ease his soul pain even in his day. We shouldn't even need to discuss worldly music any more in this chapter. You know where it belongs. Now we will give our attention to what is called religious music.

Much religious music mixes two different appeals. It has a spiritual message—a measure of it. But often it uses a type of music borrowed from the world. The effect? The music overshadows the message.

Music that is more prominent than the spiritual message of a song weakens you. To detect this problem in a song, ask yourself whether the music encourages you to pay attention to the words or whether the music gratifies you by itself.

Certainly you should enjoy music. But music that merely pleases the flesh tends to starve out spiritual interest. A casual attitude toward spiritual things sets in rather than the earnestness the believer needs to have.

Music can weaken you by making you lazy-minded. If you think you need to have music playing all the time, you probably are not really listening to it. It only trundles your mind along. Another sign of lazy-mindedness is preferring to listen rather than to sing. Only listening can be like watching someone else eat—it doesn't do you much good!

Music weakens you when it makes you prefer special singing over congregational singing. Can you enjoy the lusty heart-singing of someone who may not be on key, but who loves the Lord? Or must it have a fair degree of perfection before you like it?

How can you know which way music is affecting you? Let me suggest a few tests.

Would you be ashamed to have your parents or minister listen to all the music you listen to? Would you be glad to share all your music with your family?

Does the music move your foot more than your heart? Could you enjoy the music just as well without the words? A large part of good music is a good message.

What types of tunes do you prefer? Are they the kind that are suitable to carry a good message? The light, bouncy tunes need light, repetitious messages to fit their mood. If the words are light, they aren't doing you much good.

The singing groups you listen to—are they living out the holiness they claim to sing about? You would not support a cult such as the Mormons by buying their music. Then neither should you be putting money into the pockets of groups that are inconsistent. Besides, if you listen to such groups, it will weaken your personal conviction for living a real, consistent Christian life.

Last, we need to find out

How Music Can Strengthen You

The part of spiritual music that strengthens you is the message. The tune helps to express the mood of a song. (There is usually a difference between the tune of a funeral song and the tune of a redemption song.) The tune is the vehicle that delivers the message. You pay more attention to a letter from your friend than to the vehicle that brought it. You should do much the same with songs.

Singing strengthens us because it gives us a way to express ourselves to God and to each other. When we sing what we mean and mean what we sing, we are more convinced of it afterwards. Others who hear us are inspired too.

Singing gives us words to praise God. Be sure to praise from your heart and not only with your lips. Think of God as close by, listening to you. He is! Many songs are prayers, and we know that praying always strengthens a Christian.

Remember to pray them as you sing.

Congregational singing strengthens us more than choir or special group singing. Worshiping God in spirit and truth calls us to sing, not just to listen to it. And congregational singing does not draw more attention to the music (or the singers) than to the message.

What about musical instruments? Are they an asset to spiritual music? Do they help to convey the Bible message of truth? Should they be part of our music interests?

In the Old Testament, people used instruments for worship. But notice that they also had a tabernacle, a high priest, and endless sacrifices. Their worship had to be aesthetic (beautiful to the senses) because they did not have the kind of heart experience the New Testament believer has. The New Testament does not mention or even imply that we should use musical instruments as a means of worship today. The Bible says, "Speaking to yourselves in psalms and hymns and spiritual songs, singing and making melody in your heart to the Lord" (Ephesians 5:19).

Should recorded instrumental music also be avoided in spiritual music? Its effect is basically the same, so the value of it is just as questionable.

Some people like to play instruments for sheer enjoyment—the way others read a book. Are they in danger that way? Well, in many cases, people's interest in playing an instrument just for pleasure has been part of a more shallow, casual Christianity, rather than a real zeal for God. (Reading a book for pleasure alone also has very little value.) There are more positive ways a Christian can exercise his love for the Lord—and find real enjoyment too!

To sum it up, sing! Sing on the job or driving down the road, and by all means, sing in church. If you are not the best singer, give the group some background volume at least—enough for the Lord to know you appreciate Him. He is much more concerned that your heart is in tune with Him than whether your music is on tune.

Finally, if you want a good musical diet, you must make intelligent choices, rather than just taking in whatever comes your way. You learned to like some foods because you knew they were good for you. You rejected harmful things, and they became repulsive to you.

In the same way, deliberately guide your musical appetite. Choose only what you know is good for you. Let other spiritual people help you guide your musical appetite. Even if you do not see the dangers of some types of music, honor the wisdom of those who do.

Young man, take a good hard look at your musical appetites. Does the music you enjoy cause you to want to serve the Lord with all your heart? Or does it make you weaker and less eager to really please God and do all you can to glorify Him?

Think about it. You cannot afford less than what is best for you spiritually. Never spoil your appetite for spiritual music. God never meant for music to trap you, but to make you strong—strong for God.

Chapter 19

Your Recreation Time

Frank leaned on his shovel. "Well, are you going to the fair tomorrow?"

John looked up from his work. "No, I won't be going."

"Why not?" questioned Frank.

"I am a Christian, and I know going there would not help me on my way to heaven. I stay away from that kind of place."

"You know what, John? I'm not surprised. I've been watching you lately. I saw you don't go in for the sports and all the other stuff. Isn't your life kind of dull? What do you do evenings and in your spare time? Everybody needs some fun."

John laid his hammer aside. "You know what? Several years ago before I was a Christian, I was into those things. But now I have much more enjoyment than I ever had."

Frank shook his head. "I can't believe it. I can't believe it. But I must admit, you're one of the most content and happy fellows I ever worked with. How come?"

"It's in how you look at your life, Frank. When I was converted, Jesus became the Master of my life. Now I try to live every hour for Him whether I am at work or wherever I am. My life and my time are not my own anymore. Even what I do in my spare time is important to me."

Young man, your spare time is important too. It may well be the most influential time of your day, because you are free to choose your activity. Most of your time is probably spoken for. There must be time for sleeping, eating, and working. But then comes time for recreation. What you do when you are free and have no present responsibilities reveals your real interests and values. It also helps to establish those interests and values.

The world specializes in providing all kinds of entertainment and amusement. What it offers is strictly intended for pleasure—which means trouble for the spiritual man. You know that God has something better for you than just to live selfishly. Recreation can be a snare for a young man with lots of energy and ideas. I hope this discussion can help you find the way.

With all the wrong use of time in recreation, one might ask if recreation is really a necessary part of the Christian life. So we will start by asking,

Does a Person Need It?

Our bodies have their limits. So do our emotions. Our power of concentration is exhaustible. If we overtax ourselves, our efficiency drops. If we continue to neglect caring for our needs, it can even affect our spiritual lives.

Taking a break is a necessary part of well-being. As someone said, "If you don't come apart [from your duties], you will come apart!" Jesus told His disciples, "Come ye yourselves apart into a desert place, and rest a while: for there were many coming and going, and they had no leisure so much as to eat" (Mark 6:31).

As you can see, to be tied down too tightly to your regular duties is not good. You need time to unwind from the pressures they bring. The problem lies in how you unwind. Temptation brings the idea that you are entitled to some time purely your own, and nobody else (not even God) should be concerned what you do with it.

But wait a minute! Did the disciples on vacation do as they pleased? Did they even get their much-deserved rest? Hardly. The multitudes had followed them and had nothing to eat. The disciples ended up feeding five thousand men. After that, they had to pick up the leftovers. On top of that, Jesus put them on a ship and sent them off for a rough night of rowing. What recreation!

I think, though, that this shows God's intention for recreation: basically a change of pace and not a discharge from responsibility.

Does that mean, then, that anything not having a direct spiritual involvement is wrong? No. Physical exercise is all right. A run-down physical condition can actually affect one's spiritual condition. At times, physical exercise is good therapy for the soul.

Nevertheless the Bible says, "For bodily exercise profiteth little" (1 Timothy 4:8). So often recreation is hard on the body and causes spiritual problems. We have to look at recreation from both sides by considering

What It Can Do for You

We will talk about some of the dangers first because we want to end up on the positive side.

You need to remember that Satan always tries to spoil any potential good. He has bent the matter of recreation to his advantage. Some people say they need recreation, but end up "wrecking" themselves physically in getting it. They have to recuperate from their vacations.

Another major snare is letting recreation become the chief interest in life. I know some people who live for their vacations. From the time they get back from one vacation, they are looking forward to the next one. Some live from one ball game to the next.

Recreation is out of control when it endangers spiritual interest. One symptom is having more enthusiasm for hunting or some other activity than for spiritual exercise. If recreation gets a person more excited than the Lord's matters, something is wrong. When people have lots of energy for themselves, but are too busy or tired for the Lord, something is wrong. When people seek satisfaction for self rather than seeking first the kingdom of God, recreation has become an end in itself.

Another evidence of being overcome by recreation is when people become choosy about the type of physical activity they want. Some young men at a Bible school wanted to organize an outdoor game for recreation. They wanted a change after being in class all day. That was understandable. However, it was after a snowfall, and some sidewalks needed clearing. The administrator asked the boys to shovel the snow instead, if they needed exercise. For a few of them, the need for exercise suddenly disappeared. Why?

Young man, you must be alert lest you be overtaken by these dangers. A wrong attitude toward recreation is like a disease that takes over the whole value system. If not checked, it eats away at your desire for spiritual things. You do not want recreation to wreck you spiritually. Let me tell you what God meant recreation to do for you.

Young Man, Be Strong

First, recreation should re-create you. The man whose work strains his body needs physical rest. He should read a book or sit down to visit with a friend. The man whose work puts stress on his mind needs to ease off the mental work. He should go for a walk or cut firewood.

Whatever you do for your body, don't forget your spirit. You must find a balance that serves the whole man. Let me finish the verse about bodily exercise: "But godliness is profitable unto all things, having promise of the life that now is, and of that which is to come." Now let's see how you can help yourself become strong through recreation by

Using It Well

God wants you to treat your body right. He holds people responsible for abusing their bodies with drugs, tobacco, alcohol, and other vices. But the body and good health are not an end in themselves. Your body is to be a servant to you and God; you are not to serve it.

Thomas Edison said, "The only use for my body is to carry my brain around." If Edison thought his brain more important than his body, shouldn't we think our soul is much more important than the body?

So for recreation to really profit, you must see it as a time to favor the spiritual man. You will need to avoid those activities that are purely for the flesh. Places where the world gathers for entertainment are off limits because of their destructive power.

Does this leave room to do things for sheer enjoyment? Does the Christian have a right to do anything recreational that isn't directly related to his spiritual life? The answer to that is a cautious yes—cautious, lest it be misinterpreted as a license for the flesh. A hike, a book, a puzzle, a game, a visit, or the like can be invigorating. The more mature you become, the more mature your activity should become. Remember how Paul said, "When I was a child, I spake as a child, I understood as a child, I thought as a child: but when I became a man, I put away childish things" (1 Corinthians 13:11).

One of the marks of the Christian is temperance. Temperance is total abstinence from all that is wrong and moderation in everything that is good. There are many things which are right to do—if done at the right time, in the right place, and in the right amount. But if these things are allowed to cut into spiritual activities, they are out of proportion. For example, if they keep you from midweek Bible study, you will need to make adjustments.

Another factor is cost. Much money can be poured into recreational gadgets. It's one thing to have a usable fishing rod, but quite another thing to think you need all the gear. A neighbor once told me his tackle box contains close to a thousand dollars' worth of lures. A pair of skates is enjoyable. But must they be the best? When money is spent more easily for this kind of thing than it is put into the offering, temperance has been lost.

Check on yourself. Do you spend money for the Lord just as easily as for yourself? What if the church needs money for some emergency use and you had planned to buy another fishing rod? What do you do if you have something planned and your neighbor needs help? or help is needed in the garden at home? Can you let your preferred plan go? Another practical test: Can you have your personal devotions without thinking about your recreational interests?

You do well to mix recreation with serving others. In fact, this is the best re-creating there is, because it is very fulfilling to the soul. A helping hand, a visit, or an errand is good for you and for those you help. Always be on the lookout for such opportunities.

As to your physical recreational needs, the best place to fill them is at home. Whenever adults get together to play, it becomes self-serving rather than encouraging service.

Whatever your activity, be sure it meets the direction of Colossians 3:17. *"And whatsoever ye do in word or deed, do all in the name of the Lord Jesus, giving thanks to God and the Father by Him."* The Bible says "Jesus . . . went about doing good." Young man, if you use your free time in an unselfish way, He will become strong within you.

Chapter 20

If You Fail

Your battle against sin does not end when you become a Christian. Instead, it intensifies. You have begun to resist temptation as never before; yet Satan never gives up trying to defeat you. So you must brace yourself for a long battle against sin. How you handle that battle is our chief concern in this chapter.

The first question we must settle is

Can You Fail?

Can you sin, or can I, even after we are Christians? The answer is yes. We have the power of choice, and that means we can sin. We can even choose to go back completely into a life of sin. Frightening thought, isn't it? But it is a real possibility, and we must treat it that way. That is why the Bible gives so many warnings against it. Here is a sample from 2 Peter 2:21: "For it had been better for them not to have known the way of righteousness, than, after they have known it, to turn from the holy commandment delivered unto them."

However, we must quickly ask another question. Must

we sin? Must we fail? The answer is a resounding *no!* The Bible says, "Greater is he that is in you, than he that is in the world" (1 John 4:4).

Knowing these two facts helps you escape two of Satan's traps. He wants you to believe either that you can't sin (so that you become careless) or that you can't help but sin (so that you give up trying).

God has made it possible for us not to sin. He often tells us so. First John 2:1 says, "My little children, these things write I unto you, that ye sin not."

Yet, and I say this cautiously, while God calls believers to perfection, He knew that His children would not be perfect in all their actions. That is why He tells us the remedy if we do sin. The same verse goes on to say, "And if any man sin, we have an advocate with the Father, Jesus Christ the righteous."

It appears that every believer at one time or another needs that Advocate because of having sinned. I have never heard of anyone who needed none of God's forgiveness after he became a Christian. The big question, then, is not, "Have you ever sinned?" but "What do you do if you fail and sin?" What you do with sin tells what kind of spirit you have. The Bible says that David was a man after God's own heart. Was this because he was so perfect? Hardly! His readiness to repent and turn back to God had much to do with it. Judas did the opposite. After sinning, instead of repenting, he went out and hanged himself.

Can it happen? Yes. *Must* it happen? No. What do you do if it *does* happen??? That's the question you and I both must answer. Before we go into that, we want to talk about

What Brings Failure

Remember, young man, we are not suggesting that you must fail. But we must honestly face the possibility. Then we must work to avoid the snares that bring failure. We don't even know all the snares, but let's discuss several of them.

Obviously, temptation itself is a kind of snare. Some kinds of temptation grind away at a person's resistance—the kind we are exposed to regularly. Other temptations spring up suddenly—seemingly out of nowhere. Temptation seems to have an uncanny sense of timing—it strikes just when resistance is lagging. That is partly for the same reason that germs make us sick when our physical resistance is low. But it is also because Satan is masterminding the attack.

Spiritual decline through carelessness is a snare. A young man who starts downhill with neglect or a "don't care" attitude soon increases momentum. Prayerlessness sets in. He begins to show resentment or bitterness toward others. The snare of carelessness does not start with a sudden fall, but with a gentle glide. But it catches people just the same.

Our sinful flesh is a snare. We must guard against its lustful desires by being careful what we see, what we read, and what we think and talk about. Failure to keep those sinful desires crucified brings more failure, and temptations become even more persistent and insistent.

Overexposure to temptation brings failure. Another look, another page, or a little more time in the wrong place invites disaster. There are times when God's promised "way to escape" (1 Corinthians 10:13) is to flee. Proverbs asks, "Can a man take fire in his bosom, and his clothes not be burned?" The implied answer is no!

Disappointments and difficulties can be a snare. Perhaps death takes someone close to you. You need to cope with the painful emptiness. It is easy to respond wrongly at a time like that. Or you may have had some cherished dream shattered. Perhaps a friendship, a job, or some other opportunity has passed you by. Do you go down in self-pity and discouragement?

Relationships with other people can cause you difficulty. You may be misunderstood or mistreated. Resentment can build up—especially toward those with authority over us. You may be tempted to complain, "What he said might have been right, but I couldn't stand the way he said it!"

Overtaxed emotions can trap you. When you are tired, little things become big things. So can uncontrolled emotions (temper). I saw one man get so exasperated at a tool that was not working quite right that he took a sledge hammer and smashed it.

Or perhaps he fell into the trap of thinking that life owed him certain things. Another man who worked in the same shop handled setbacks and difficulties so graciously that I marveled at him. One day I asked him how he could stay so calm under the pressure. He said, "You can't fight it. You gotta roll with the punches." He meant that we have to accept those things we cannot change.

The snare of depression is becoming increasingly widespread. Recently it was said that depression is the most important difficulty that doctors deal with. No doubt many people fall during a time of depression. They might turn on God and blame Him for their problems.

Doubt and unbelief walk hand in hand with depression. Satan is always trying to drive people to despair and a "what's the use? I give up" feeling. Succumbing to these temptations most certainly brings failure.

Satan often sets two snares in a row. After he has caught

us in the first one and gotten us to sin, he tries to make us wallow in despondency or guilt for a while. True, sometimes we might fall and not be able to explain why. We might be surprised at ourselves and think, "I never thought I would do something like that!" It can be terribly disappointing.

But what shall we do then? Shall we go down deeper and deeper or be mired in despondency? The only Christian answer is that by God's grace we will find our way out of failure and go on with Him.

Quick Recovery

We are interested in recovering when we fail, aren't we? We don't want to be destroyed by failure. The quicker we recover, the better.

I have to think of the water heater we had when I was a boy. Saturday night was a bad night for that water heater. It was even worse for those of us who didn't get to take a bath first. The water heater couldn't keep up with the demand, and it let us know in a chilling way.

Then "quick recovery" water heaters came along and solved the problem. They could heat the water faster than you could tap it. Then it didn't matter how much you drained from it.

Now a water heater is made to be drained. God didn't design you to be constantly drained by failure. But it's good to know that if you do fail, you can be restored as instantly as a quick-recovery water heater.

The secret to a quick recovery is to be connected to a good source of power. That power is, of course, God. Too often, when people get into spiritual trouble, they fail to tap into this source. "Oh, what peace we often forfeit, / Oh, what needless pain we bear, / All because we do not carry / Everything to God in prayer!"

Earlier you read how to keep in contact with God. Here are some more suggestions, especially for times when you fail.

First, you must care when you fail—care enough to want to get back on track with God and to be restored again spiritually. Not later or tomorrow, but you must be ready to do it right now. You can't be like the man who said, "I'm not done being mad yet." Victory comes to those who stop in their tracks when they know they are going wrong.

You must repent. (Or did you think you left repentance behind you when you were converted?) The only way back to God is the way you left. Do not hesitate to say, "I was wrong. I am sorry." If you excuse yourself, you will only make yourself smaller. Be big enough to see where you went wrong—and do something about it.

You need to exercise faith. Even if you have sinned and acted very foolishly, believe that God wants you back and is eager to accept your repentance. Then you must accept yourself and go on living again. This is very important to your recovery.

When we weld a broken scythe or plowshare in the shop, the broken spot we weld is stronger than it was before. If you break faith with God by sinning, that is, of course, very bad. But if you work together with God to mend the break, your friendship with Him can be stronger than ever. Not even an angel can love God like someone whom God has forgiven.

Then, remember those who are pulling for you. They are ready to help you get going again. Go to them when you are struggling. Your parents, ministry, and other spiritual people are the ones who can usually help you the best.

Young man, how is it with you if you sin? Do you hasten

back to your heavenly Father in true repentance? Are you ready to do your part to avoid the same pitfall again? Do you claim the promise of forgiveness which is given in 1 John 1:9? Do you then go on with renewed determination to be faithful to God?

If you can say yes to these questions, you are becoming strong. You are learning that God can turn even failure into victory.

Chapter 21

Learning to Manage Money

Once there was a man who through family ties got a farm for almost nothing. In spite of this, his relatives still had to make periodic payments to the local equipment dealer for machinery and repairs. Even with all this help, he had a hard time.

Meanwhile, other farmers were making payments on their farms and paying other bills besides, and yet they were making it without any help. What made the difference?

The difference was economics—the way people handle money and possessions. Some people seem naturally to have more business sense than others. Also, some people seem to have more opportunities. But everyone, whether he has much native ability and many opportunities or not, can help himself if he follows some basic guidelines.

This chapter will not tell you how to get rich. But it should help you to be a good steward over what God enables you to have. You do not need to be a big financial success to be a strong man for God. But God does ask you to be faithful in your finances. In fact, the matter will be considered in judgment.

Economics touches more than money and things. It affects you spiritually as well. You can't ignore the rights and wrongs of handling money and at the same time do well as a Christian. Many a man has met spiritual disaster because he failed to be totally Christian in his economic and financial life.

Money is powerful. Either you control it or it controls you. In the world, money brings prestige and position. Pursuing it, men lie and cheat. They may even steal and kill for it.

That may seem far from us. And we hope it is. But the Bible has a lot to say about money being the source of wrongdoing. Take this verse: "For the love of money is the root of all evil: which while some coveted after, they have erred from the faith, and pierced themselves through with many sorrows" (1 Timothy 6:10). How true!

Is it the amount of money that produces the evil? Not necessarily. It is the *love* of money—the *desire* for it that takes people the wrong way. The verse before the one quoted says, "But they that will [want to] be rich fall into temptation and a snare, and into many foolish and hurtful lusts, which drown men in destruction and perdition."

As you can see, it isn't only those with money who can have the problem. A person who has nothing can be just as guilty of this as the millionaire.

On the other hand, money has a lot of potential for good. God gives it in order to give us a way to serve Him. He has plans for how we should use it.

To be strong spiritually, you must pay attention to some Bible principles concerning economics. One of these is

Thrift

Thrift does not mean getting more money; it means saving the money you have. No matter how much money some

173

people get, they can't keep it. One man said, "They say money talks, but all it ever said to me was good-bye." But a mature man can walk through a store with a wallet of money and buy only what he came for. The amount of money you earn is not nearly so important as the amount you have left over when you have stopped buying.

Thrift means not only saving money, but also saving and taking care of things. Have you ever noticed how one man can get lots more out of a sheet of plywood than others—or out of a dollar—or out of a set of tires?

An employer had an operator on an expensive machine. The machine was constantly broken down and needed many, many repairs. The owner concluded it was worn out and had to be replaced. Then his operator quit, so he hired another man. Suddenly the machine worked well. Production increased drastically. The owner said you couldn't believe it was the same machine.

Both men knew how to run the machine, but they did it differently. One would jerk and bang the machine around while the other was gentle and smooth. One didn't care and thought the machine should take the beating he gave it; the other wanted to coax all he could from the machine without abusing it.

The big difference was in their attitudes. Which man do you think was constantly grumbling about everything?

At home on the farm, my father would send us boys out to pick up the ears of corn that the corn picker missed. It was slow, tedious work. We would try to persuade Father that the amount of corn we got was not worth the time—or the hard work!

Father's answer (which he said he got from his father) was, "The Lord made it grow, and we are responsible to take care of it." I see now that he cared not only about his corn, but also about teaching the right attitude to his boys.

While thrift may not appear to be the fastest way to success, it is the soundest. Being too much in a hurry to look after little things catches up with a person. "A stitch in time saves nine" is still true. "A penny saved" is still "a penny earned"—and you don't have to pay income tax on that kind of earning!

On the other hand, being careless and destructive can work havoc. Not only does it rob us of what we own, but it also becomes a bad habit. It can affect the way we treat our clothes, our cars, and maybe even our friends. It seems to invade one's whole system and even affect the spiritual life. But if we are careful with money and things, it encourages us to be careful in other areas of life also.

Another important side to handling money needs your attention. That is

Industriousness

With all the problems of greed and covetousness, maybe the answer is to avoid earning money? Perhaps slackness and laziness have some merit after all? No, no, of course not! The Bible teaches the virtue of being busy.

When God created Adam and Eve, He assigned Adam to dress and keep the Garden of Eden. Even before they sinned, they needed to work. After they sinned, God increased their workload—again for their good. He knew that more work would help them to cope with the results of their sinfulness.

Work is good for the body. It produces strength and vigor. It keeps the body healthy and comfortable. It produces a sense of well-being and usefulness. Without exercise, the body cannot function at its best.

Work is good for the soul too. It helps to occupy the mind constructively. It provides emotional release and relaxation. It brings satisfaction and a healthy outlook on life. You know what it is like to have worked hard and feel good all over.

People tend to operate at similar levels spiritually and physically. The person who can barely get out of bed and to his work has a problem getting to his Bible. If he can't discipline himself to work, he has problems dealing with spiritual struggles.

Just a caution. While being industrious is tied to spiritual life, it is not always a sign of spirituality. People can be industrious for selfish reasons.

Did you ever think about the kind of men God called to do His work? Were they loafing around? Moses and David were out back, faithfully caring for the sheep. Elisha was plowing with the other servants. Peter, James, and John were tending their nets. Jesus called the busy men.

Once the church needed workers to help in a mission project. An older brother who was in charge of recruiting the help said, "With horses, when you need more performance, you hit the one who is already pulling the hardest." People who are busy are often the only ones who have time to do more!

Of course, you can't be really industrious unless you have something to be enthusiastic about. Learn to see life as a challenge so that you can approach it with zest. Put your energies into the right things—the things you know please God. If God is enthusiastic about them, why shouldn't we be?

Thrift and industriousness make a good pair. Now we

can go on and think about

Handling Money

If I had never driven a vehicle, would you advise me to start with a tractor trailer truck? Hardly. You'd probably recommend that I take a pickup truck (preferably an old one) and practice out back somewhere. You would say that it's better to start with a small unit because that would help to get me ready to handle a big one.

I think it works that way with money too. A young person needs supervision in learning to handle money. If he doesn't get it, it's easy come, easy go. The money disappears as fast as it appears—and sometimes faster. If he doesn't learn a better habit early in life, the pattern is hard to break.

A friend of ours took her neighbor along shopping. When they got to town, the neighbor said, "Here, you take this money. I want to save it, but if I have it, it will burn holes in my pocket until I spend it." She had not learned saving habits when she was younger.

We will pause a moment here to settle a key question. When a growing young man earns money, whose money is it? Is it his own? One father said, "My son earned that money, so I have nothing to say as to what he does with it. It's his business." Was he right?

Let me explain why your money is partly your parents' business. Handling money is an important part of anybody's growing up. Because of its far-reaching effects, your parents owe it to you to help you, just as they would in other areas. They would be wrong to let you make it hard for yourself or even ruin yourself.

Does this mean that parents have the right to expect their children to give a portion of their earnings or time during their teenage years? While there are different ways of doing it, I believe that one way or another it should be done.

You owe it to your parents. They invested much money in you over the years. They are entitled to some return from you. But it is not primarily that parents feel their children owe them so much. Rather, it's a matter of respect and appreciation from you. You should also count it a privilege to help meet the needs of the whole family—not just your own needs.

I know of several young men belonging to a poor family that moved to America. Even though those brothers were grown up, they gave all their earnings to the family, with no strings attached.

That idea may seem too tight to some young people who are accustomed to a lot of freedom with the money they earn. Just remember that some of those who had a lot of freedom and a lot of money have a lot less now than some others whose parents kept a close rein on their money. The money they once had has slipped through their fingers. Worse yet, they have not learned how to handle money.

As I mentioned, learning to handle money can start at an early age. The penny bank idea is a good one. I hope you learned the value of saving pennies, nickels, and dimes instead of spending them for candy and soda. Even though it may take a long time to save as much as an adult earns in a day, there is tremendous value in it.

I was reminded of that the other day when I took one of the children's savings to the bank. The coins and crinkled bills amounted to twenty dollars! True, that might not sound like much to an adult. But, as the mother of one of my friends told him, "A lot of pennies make a dollar." I like another saying: "If you save your pennies, your dollars will take care of themselves." Until a person has learned the value of small amounts, he is not safe with large ones.

So what should a young man do if no one holds the line for him? What could the young man have done whose father said it was none of his business how his son spends his money? I would suggest that he voluntarily subject himself to a responsible adult who can help him learn how to use money.

It is healthy to want to save money. While the amount may seem to grow slowly, remember, it is still there. Since you don't know what you might do with it in the future, you may think, "Why bother to save?" Let me assure you of one thing: if you save money, you will be glad you did. Let me assure you of another thing too: if you don't, you will wish you had. Sooner than you think, perhaps, you will want to buy a house of your own. That's just one example.

So far in this chapter, we have discussed earning and saving. A third very important thing is still missing. Let me tell you about a man who was listening to a sermon about money. The preacher's first point was, "Get all you can." The second was, "Save all you can." The listener looked at a friend approvingly and said, "That's what I always tried to do." But the third point, "Give all you can," floored him. How disappointed he was. But without the last point, the other two are dangerous.

Sometimes young people think the older people of the church are more obligated to give to the Lord in offerings than the young. They think they will give more when they get older too. But when is it easier to start giving—when there are family responsibilities, or when there are none? Does God expect a smaller portion of your earnings just because you are young? I'm sure that with a bit of thinking, you know the answer to these questions.

Now let's take a more detailed look at your spending habits. Do you try to buy everything you'd like to have? Just because you have the money does not justify buying everything you might like. You have probably discovered that if you have money, it takes more grit not to buy than to buy.

Do you always need the best? Why do you need a car or a pickup truck—for practical reasons or for status? Do not be like the young man of whom it was said, "He wants more than just a car." Should a young man pour his life savings into something that in a few years will be worn out? In times of prosperity and affluence, a Christian needs to ask himself some sober questions.

Avoid buying just to keep up with others. It's amazing how easy it is to think you need something just because others have it. You can end up buying more clothes, gadgets, or even tools than you need. Even if you do need a camera or recording equipment, you should look for something with a practical price tag.

God may have real blessings for someone through the money you save. Suppose a brother in the church has a fire or a big hospital bill. How encouraged he would be if you would offer him a low-interest or no-interest loan! Or the church may need to build an annex or a school. Your money can bless many people if you make it available.

What about investing, let's say in some livestock of your own, or in your uncle's new business? What about investing in a house?

When you invest, never do it recklessly. Quick moves are often regretted. Ask advice from people who have more experience. Then be ready to take it. Avoid the get-rich-quick approach.

Young man, remember that it isn't those who hoard their money who are the most useful to God. Neither is it those who spend their money too freely. It is those who seek to apply Bible principles to their financial life. Determine to use your money and resources to God's honor and glory. You will be putting them into the bank of heaven. The interest will make you strong.

Chapter 22

What Should You Work?

The local high school where I grew up published an annual yearbook. It had a picture of each of the graduates and a description of them. My favorite part of this was what the graduate said he wanted to be and accomplish in life. I often wonder how many of them reached their vocational goals.

You are probably past the "When I get big, I'm going to be . . ." stage by now. Dreaming time is over, and it's time to work. For some young men, a particular slot is already waiting. But perhaps you still need to make a choice. What should you work?

I am not planning to try to tell you what to work. But there are some things about working that affect you spiritually. These are things you will want to sort through carefully, because no one can afford to let his work drag him down spiritually.

Since we discussed the value of working earlier, we can go on now to more specifics. One of them is the question, should you be zeroing in on a particular occupation at this time and specializing in it? In answer let me point out the

Value of Varied Skills

It is good for a young man to be versatile. Sometimes knowing something about mechanics is more valuable than being the best tradesman. It is very unhandy to be a highly skilled person and yet not know how to change a flat tire. Our local garage man says that the most professional people in town know the least about taking care of their cars.

There are many other places where a little know-how is good. Not needing to get an electrician to change a fuse is a real advantage, isn't it? And just because you aren't a carpenter doesn't mean there isn't any value in being able to build something.

You never know what skills you might need in life. My cousin was a good mechanic and ran a repair shop right next to us. It was quite handy to let him do our repair work. That was fine for both of us. However, some years later we moved away to a more remote area, and he didn't. I had become so dependent that the adjustment to doing things myself was painful.

Should everybody be a "Jack of all trades"? Not necessarily. But for a young man, it's good to be a practical person. Discipline yourself to be a good learner in the practical skills. Who knows—the skill you now think unnecessary may be just what you need later in life.

Finally, though, you need to settle down to a regular type of work. Before we discuss choosing such an occupation, we must recognize that

Occupations Can Be Dangerous

Of course, we know that some occupations are dangerous to a worker's back or lungs or skin. But we want to look at ways they might damage a man's relationship with the Lord.

There is a danger that a man might want a particular occupation for the sake of prestige. He might want to be rich and powerful, or at least highly thought of. His occupation may be a subtle way of exalting self.

There is the danger of getting involved too deeply in one's occupation. This can be a special problem for young men because of all the enthusiasm they often have. Some of them pour all their physical and mental energies into their work. It seems to be all they can talk or think about.

With priorities mixed up like this, people find it very difficult to give spiritual matters first place. They may be overworked and too tired to be really involved in a worship service. They might not even get there. ("I planned to, but things did not hold out.") They can hardly take time out to help someone in need. They also tend to neglect their personal time with the Lord.

There is nothing righteous about working too hard. Work is part of our duty in life, but not the primary part. Guard against giving all your best energies to your occupation. The Lord has better things than that!

Another danger in some occupations is what they can do to family life. When work comes first, it can rob the family of having enough time together. It can keep Father away from home too many evening or even nights. Discipline quickly suffers. Family worship time might be crammed into a few minutes or crowded out altogether.

Any occupation is dangerous when it encourages pride. A highly trained professional man wanted to become a member of the church. The ministry met with him regularly to instruct him in the faith. One evening he was quite frustrated when he came. He said the devil was telling him all day how foolish it was for him to let himself be instructed by some men with so much less training than he had. He didn't take the devil's advice. But it was a temptation.

You may become more skilled in some way than your parents. Sometimes young men think that makes them wiser than their parents all around. It doesn't. It doesn't make them superior to anyone else either, for that matter. Don't let your occupation become a snare of pride to you.

This certainly does not complete the list of potential dangers. But it should help you carefully examine the dangers of whatever line of work you are considering. Let's go on and look at

Choosing an Occupation

There is no real hurry for a teenager to have an occupation all lined up. This is the time to learn the disciplines of work and the general skills. I'm not encouraging job hopping, because learning to stick to something is valuable in itself. But do not feel that you must have your life work laid out before you now. In His own good time, God will lead you into the occupation He knows is good for you. Here are some of the ways He might lead you.

Circumstances and opportunity often influence a young man's choice. Many sons follow their father's footsteps because they have the opportunity to get involved in their father's work. They also learn to appreciate the benefits that particular occupation provides.

Another aspect is personal preference. One young man thinks mechanical work is great. He prefers the grease to some dusty job his friend has. His friend feels just as good about his own job. That is all right, because God gave us different preferences. A person ought to be able to enjoy his occupation. Most occupations have their less desirable sides that one accepts and endures. But usually a person should not dread the day's work.

A factor closely related to this is aptitude—what you are naturally good at. Some young men can operate a machine smoothly but can barely pound a nail in straight, while others are the opposite. Some young men prefer to work their minds harder than their bodies, and some prefer the other way around—likely because they are better at one than the other.

So you say you have a preference and know your ability. What if there is no place to put these two to work? A third criterion is opportunity. Sometimes God doesn't provide what you think you prefer to work. Don't be impatient and waste your life wishing and waiting for the perfect opportunity. Accept what is most practical at the moment. Many of the best opportunities have come while a person was faithful where he was.

Something else to keep in mind is the availability of work. Some trades and skills are always in demand. If you stay in the realm of the essential services (providing food, shelter, and so forth), you will usually find work available. The apostle Paul had a tentmaking trade that served him well wherever he went. As he said in Titus 3:14, "Let ours also learn to maintain good works for necessary uses, that they be not unfruitful."

Obviously, this rules out taking a job in the entertainment and amusement world. It also rules out involvement in the armed forces and in making body-damaging products such as liquor, tobacco, and narcotics. Types of businesses that produce luxuries for the rich come into serious question. The antique business would be one of these.

Consider the environment in which you must work. Even a good occupation cannot be good for you if you must work side by side with foul-mouthed or evil-hinting men (or women). Sacrifice dollars, if you must, to work with those who will not undermine your faith.

Perhaps it seems as if job decisions are already made for you. Necessity at home, for example, can keep you working at a particular job. Accept that for now and trust God to open other doors if it is His will.

Remember, what your occupation is does not matter nearly so much as what it does to you and others spiritually. Make that your chief concern. This means we should say

A Word About Professions

Can an occupation be too professional? Or should the Christian seek to excel in the professional world of medicine, politics, law, or banking? Many people say that this is what society needs. Who would be a better candidate for a profession than a young man of good character? That may sound logical, but the question is not really so simple.

The professions often make demands that reduce one's power to serve the Lord elsewhere. A professional tends to pour his time, energy, and mental powers into his profession. Sometimes it is said that these professions offer unique opportunities to serve the Lord. The fact is, many times the pressure of the profession puts the spiritual ministry into the background. In many cases, even missionary doctors and teachers who have served their profession well have not been successful in promoting the Lord's cause.

Another threat of the professions is that they put a person into the company of professionals. The social pressure to fit into the mold of that profession is great. Being their equal in the world often confuses the Biblical lines of separation for the Christian. Then he can easily lose his identity as a Christian. When a Christian doctor looks into the mirror, does he see a Christian, or does he see . . . a doctor?

The spiritual casualty rate among professionals is too high to consider the professions safe.

Does this mean, then, that God wants us to let our mental powers lie dormant and undeveloped? Of course not! It means that God has something more eternal for us to give ourselves to. One young man, for example, heard a strong invitation to give his mind and energies to the causes of this world. Universities looked attractive. Instead, he chose to give himself to teaching in a Christian school.

God has ways for every believer to use all the mental energies he has. There is a great need for teachers—in the church and in the Christian school. The need for Bible students who know what and why they believe has never been greater. Neither is the need for Christian writers any less. There is something for every believer to do. God has something for you to do.

God calls us to excellence. But the first chapter of 1 Corinthians tells us, "Not many wise men after the flesh, not many mighty, not many noble, are called." (It would be worth your time to read the whole context of this verse in chapters 1 and 2.) God's program in the world does not depend on the professionals of the day. Rather, He tells us that He uses those of low esteem.

Joseph understood this principle. When he brought his family down to Egypt, he had the power to give them whatever he chose. What did he give them? Was it the royalty and the best Egypt had to offer? No! He told his family to tell the Egyptians they were shepherds. Why, since shepherds were despised in Egypt? No. Because he understood the power of occupational pressures.

You are influenced by what your father has worked at. My father had polio when he was a child. This handicapped his walking. The local banker put a lot of pressure on my grandfather to let my father take up banking as a career. My grandfather refused. No doubt my father and the rest of the family would be in a vastly different situation if that environment had become part of our lives.

We should touch business ventures here. As a young man, you need not be in a hurry to be your own boss. You can learn valuable lessons by working your way up from the bottom rather than jumping into business for yourself. You might even discover that the pressures and complexities of business would be too much of a drain for you. Not everybody is cut out to handle the headaches of managing a business. Maybe you can be more useful in another place. Be satisfied to serve the Lord in whatever way He opens the door for you.

Young man, use your occupation as a way to serve the Lord. Don't sacrifice eternal values for a little of this old world. Remember that the type of work you do doesn't decide whether or not you are great. It's the God you work for that counts. Make it count for eternity.

Chapter 23

Developing Your Personality

In many people, personality is only skin deep. A salesman came to see our neighbor. He gave the neighbor a pen as part of his gracious introduction. But, in spite of all his efforts, the neighbor didn't buy. Finally the salesman gave up. While leaving, he deftly reclaimed the pen from the neighbor's shirt pocket! When the smiles and gimmicks failed, another side came out.

Or, if you please, some people's personalities are like cotton candy—nice and big, but with very little substance. It's only a clever fluff-up job. The charm and happiness they show in public can go to nothing at home.

Two children approached their father while he was studying. He let them know that he had no time for them and curtly sent them away. The hurt children asked their mother what Father was doing to make him so grouchy. The answer? Their salesman father was studying how to be nice to the people in town!

That sounds quite unfair, doesn't it? But it might come closer to us than we think. I know of a mother who told her spatting boys that she could not understand how they could suddenly become so pleasant when company came. Do you think only young boys have that problem?

We are not trying to get into a personality polishing session such as the world promotes. But God has given us personalities for a reason. How we develop our personalities is important to Him and to us.

So far, we have seen only the poor side of personality. Now we shall see

What Personality Is

Let's start by comparing personality and character. Earlier we emphasized that character is what we are on the inside—underneath the surface. Personality is more on the surface and visible to others. It is supposed to be the expression of our character. God designed our personality to be the window through which others can see what is on the inside of us. Christian personality is like a deep, clear pool in which you can see the bottom and yet hardly realize how deep the water really is.

But God wants the personality to be more than just a window. He also wants the personality to be the door through which He, the indwelling One, can come out and show Himself to the world in real flesh and blood. Colossians 3:6–16 tells us how the old man must be put off and the new man (who is like God) must be put on.

Since the personality is more like a clear window than a wall, what is on the inside is by far the most important. Most of our discussions so far emphasized that. But once we have the new man within us, it is only fair to make sure our personality is pleasant, so it can express the Christian character within.

This is far different from polishing up the outside to hide

what is inside. The Christian does not try to refine his personality for selfish advantage (as a salesman might do). Rather, he does it to let God express Himself through him. Any other reason would take him trespassing into the world's realm of image polishing.

Improving our personalities does not mean we should all try to have *the one perfect personality*. There is no such thing. Some people are gentle and easygoing; others are more aggressive. Some can laugh off failure; others are sensitive even to the failures of friends. Some get things done in a hurry; others are perfectionists. Most of us are a curious mixture of traits that make us different from anyone else.

God did not intend for us all to be exactly alike. Aren't you glad? It is said that people who are too much alike have to work harder at getting along well with each other. If so, imagine a world full of people who are all alike!

God didn't plan for us to be complete without the balance of others. He didn't even create Adam that way. All the good personality traits mentioned above have their weaknesses which other people can counterbalance. Mild people enjoy having someone with a lively personality pop in and add some spice to their day.

Jesus gathered several personality types around Him. There were outspoken Peter and the two sons of Thunder who were ready to call fire down from heaven when provoked. Then there were others who shone in their quiet, meditative, and reflective ways. Together they became a mighty band for the Master.

But don't expect other people to balance you off to the point that you don't have to work on your own personality. An aggressive, outgoing person, if he is not careful, can be very offensive to others. A person whose strength lies in being quiet and receding may find it hard to exert himself when he knows he should. We should recognize these particular tendencies in ourselves and try to improve them. We should not say, "This is how I am. I've always been like this. So don't try to change me. Why, my father even . . ."

No. Maybe you alone can't improve the rough spots in your personality, but God can. Instead of wishing you were someone else, take a good look at yourself and ask (not as if you were accusing God), "Why has God given me the disposition I have? What are the areas I need to be developing in?" Though painful, this can be rewarding.

Perhaps you are aggressive and emotional. If so, perhaps sometimes you state your case too emphatically without considering the feelings of others. Do you listen to them only with the idea of changing their minds, or are you open to them?

Maybe you are the kind who is seldom heard. Could it be that you should contribute more to others? Often the quiet ones have thought more than the talkers!

If you are the easygoing type who mixes easily, beware. You might be swept along in the wrong way. Be careful whom you expose yourself to, and keep your guards up.

While we are interested in improving our own personalities, we need to resist the temptation to try to change other people to make them more desirable to us. We should appreciate what we can in other people that is different from us and contributes to our lives.

One very important force greatly affects the personality and will cause much difficulty if not handled properly. To avoid this difficulty, we must learn about

Harnessing the Emotions

Emotions are our feelings—happiness, grief, anger, and calmness. They are valuable and make life interesting. Who wants to go to a wedding or a funeral without feeling the stirring of emotion? That would be like being unable to taste. If you could not taste, you would envy people who could taste even bitter things.

Emotions can be extremely powerful. You have probably heard stories of people who during a house fire carried big, heavy things to safety that they could never have carried any other time. Emotions got their adrenalin working! But that same power gets people into big trouble. You probably also know of people who in anger did or said things they regretted for years.

But, in an everyday way, emotions affect our lives even more. They color our outlook. They affect how big a job looks. One day a particular chore might look formidable to us. The next day it might seem like a breeze. Naturally, this affects how much we actually get done.

Emotional upsets, although they begin in the nervous system, affect the rest of the body. If allowed to run on too long, they can throw our delicately balanced make-up out of line. When this happens, medical help may be needed.

The Christian wants his emotions to help him *feel,* and yet he does not want his feelings to become his master. He wants to be in touch with his surroundings, but not be ruled by them. He wants to feel the joy of his relationship with God, but at the same time not trust alone in his feelings.

Our emotions seldom perform in such a balanced way without intelligent guidance. Those of us who tend to let our feelings govern us must learn to harness our feelings.

We can be thankful that the Lord of all is able to be the Lord of our emotions.

An important part of emotional control is self-discipline. That means you can't always do how you feel. Your parents probably taught you some painful lessons about that in years gone by. (At least I hope you had that privilege.) Instead of allowing your emotions to dictate your actions, your will must decide that you will act right, whether you feel like it or not. Interestingly, though, you can then learn to enjoy the blessing of doing what you know you should. Even your emotions will feel good about that!

Last, here is a bit of

Practical Advice

It would be easy to say that being a true Christian is all that you need in order to have the right kind of personality. While that is essential, your personality requires growth and development. Seldom does it happen that no details need individual attention.

Even though the Holy Spirit is in your heart, you need to cultivate the fruit of the Spirit. Study carefully how love, joy, peace, long-suffering, gentleness, goodness, faith, meekness, and temperance ought to be expressed in your life. (That might make a good theme for personal devotions.) Making yourself aware of how those ought to be expressed could produce a major improvement in your heart and then in your personality. Every time I work through that list, the Holy Spirit is busy showing me areas that can use improvement.

Living by the Golden Rule certainly goes a long way in making you what you should be. To have a pleasant personality, concentrate on the good of others, rather than on yourself. Count it a privilege to live for the good of others.

Young Man, Be Strong

Be yourself. You don't need to blow yourself up bigger than you really are in front of others, nor do you need to constantly run yourself down before others. And don't try to imitate other people. If you see desirable traits in others, ask God to help you to become more like that. You need to accept yourself, and yet never be quite satisfied with yourself, because you always want to grow.

Be genuine. Some people are always so loudly happy that you wonder if it's for real. Don't feel, either, that you must be everything to everybody. That would wear you out—and likely wear them out too.

At the same time, don't express every feeling that crosses your mind. There is a time to be pleasant to your family and neighbors even if you don't feel that way. To be genuine, bring your feelings into line with the way you should act.

In conversation, be truly interested in others. After church, you don't need to stand around and wait for others to come to you. Make the move to talk with the less talkative. And don't just talk about yourself. Ask questions sometimes. Try to understand what the other person is saying rather than just waiting for a chance to get started again. Look him in the eye, rather than looking around at other attractions.

Be demonstrative. Don't be afraid to show your appreciation. Do your little brothers (or big ones) know you appreciate them? Do your parents know? What do you say if your sister bakes your favorite cake? You don't need to be gushy and make a lot of fuss about things. But don't assume that people know your feelings without being told. Don't be like the man who, it is said, told his wife on their wedding day, "I love you, and I'll tell you if it ever changes." Keep it fresher than that!

In social life, don't ignore those you don't know. If

someone new is present, take the initiative to get acquainted. You probably know how it feels not to know anyone and how glad you are for someone who breaks the ice with you. Be careful about sticking with your best friends too much. True, some people are easier to visit with. You seem to click with them. But then it's tempting to let a real clique develop. Of course, most people have friends who are closer to them than others. But we must avoid treating some people as if they aren't important to us. Christian love can take in a lot of people—everybody. Be modest in expressing yourself. Let others have the last word. You don't need to top someone else's story or tell a funnier happening. Rather, be concerned that your life gives a testimony of serious Christian living.

Consider the Christian virtues you appreciate in others. Check yourself against those good virtues, and make an honest effort to grow where you are coming up short. Be alert to the hints others may drop about how you might be more considerate or mature.

Always look out for the good of others. While the world polishes the outside for personal gain, you have a much higher goal. It is, "Thou shalt love thy neighbor as thyself."

Determine to let God mold your personality after Himself. Seek for the right way to let Him shine in you. Desire to be the blessing to others that He counts on you to be. And development of your personality will be one of the results.

Chapter 24

Don't Be Obnoxious

The Bible says that Jesus grew in "wisdom and stature, and in favour with God and man." Apparently Jesus had manners that made Him acceptable to people around Him.

Much of this book emphasizes growing in favor with God. In this chapter we will discuss practical ways you can grow in favor with men. The young man who wants to be strong for the Lord has to behave in a way worthy of the Lord.

There is more than one wrong kind of personality. For example, Arnold is so slick and polished it is distasteful. Somehow he seems too artificial; he makes you wonder what he expects out of the people he treats so smoothly. His politeness and courtesy look rather effeminate. It just does not radiate genuine Christian virtue. He seems almost too nice.

On the other hand, Sam always seems a little backward. Without a doubt, his heart is in the right place. His sincerity shines through. But it is a little hard for him to fit into group conversations and activities. When he does exert himself, it is difficult for others to know how to react. It seems he never thinks of any way of doing things except the way they do it at home. Sometimes he feels a little out of place and awkward, but does not know what to do about it.

These may be two extremes, I know. But I suspect that you and I both have had Sam's difficulty along the way. At the same time, we want to exercise the Christian graces without coming across like Arnold did. There must be a balance that demonstrates true Christian strength.

Really, I don't expect to tell you many new things. What I am promoting is just old-fashioned common sense dosed with love. Refresh your memory here, and test yourself a bit. We can get a little careless and inconsiderate if we don't pay attention to these areas.

Let me first remind you to

Mind Your Mannerisms

Mannerisms are little habits of doing things, such as the way you respond to others—with a grunt or a thank-you. They include the little unconscious gesture, the nervous twitch, the loud *haawwh-aarrggh* when you clear your throat, or the high-pitched squeal that accompanies your sneeze.

Not all mannerisms are totally obnoxious. Who would want to take Grandpa's special chuckle from him? But you might want to take a critical look at your own habits.

Sometimes we think we can't change our annoying habits. Granted, the longer you wait to attack a bad habit, the harder it is to get rid of it. But bad habits can be changed if you are serious about it.

How?

First you must recognize them. This can be hard, because we can't see ourselves. There was a man whose wife had a problem with the way he ate (or sucked) soup. He just could not understand why it was so offensive to her. One day he was at a public eating place. A woman nearby was eating soup. She would put the spoon to her mouth and there would be a *ffflllipppp* sound and the soup was gone. Suddenly he understood, because he saw it in someone else. His wife's problem was solved—although he had to work to change his habit.

You might not conquer a bad habit just by realizing what you are doing wrong. But realizing it is the first step. From then on, a reminder flag waves when you do it again. Some public speakers have had listeners who pointed out some distracting speaking habits (such as saying *okay* quite often). While the habits don't stop immediately, the speakers said that when they did it again, they thought about it. Before, they had done it again and again and never thought of it.

Since we can be offensive to others and scarcely be aware of it, we must rely on others to point out our problems. And while we may question their sensitivity, we must admit that other people besides ourselves have opinions on what is pleasant or offensive. In short, we must learn to

Think of Others

True courtesy is born when we learn to consider others. Some people say, "I don't care what anybody thinks. This is how I do it." If they lived somewhere in the wilderness, that would be their privilege. But since we live among other people, we owe it to them and to ourselves to consider their expectations and observe the usual courtesies.

Remember the common courtesies of "please," "thank you," "pardon me," and the like. Make them a matter of habit so that you use them without thinking. Do not be like the speaker who was earnestly telling a group about the importance of saying, "excuse me." As he moved around behind the speaker's stand, he accidentally stepped on the foot of the moderator, who was seated behind him. His response—"oops"—showed how easy it is to forget proper manners if you haven't practiced them. Your home is the best place for you to develop the habit.

Speaking clearly and distinctly is also being considerate. Don't mumble and jumble your words and sentences together. Depending on whom you are talking to, you may have to slow down. One time I was talking to a foreigner who arrested me with, "You speak s-o-o rapidly." Looking at the person you are talking to is also helpful.

Words are powerful and need to be used carefully. Learn to use proper grammar. (Instead of saying "me and John," say, "John and I.") While the accent of the community we live in may rub off on us, the vain and suggestive language of the world does not belong in the Christian's vocabulary at all. The Bible says, "Let no corrupt communication proceed out of your mouth, but that which is good to the use of edifying, that it may minister grace unto the hearers" (Ephesians 4:29).

You need to be aware of local manners. When traveling, you will find that customs differ. It is only courteous to try to find a level of conduct that does not offend the people you are with. In some cultures, a hearty belch after a meal indicates your approval of the meal, while in others, belching is considered to be very unmannerly. In the same way, if the people you are with do not eat bread or applesauce when you are used to eating them, don't hesitate to do as they do.

There are, of course, various acceptable ways of eating. But there are other ways that are definitely not acceptable. To be safe, remember that simply thinking of others first at the table will go a long way toward suitable manners. Also, remember that you are not in a speed contest. Eating with friends has more noble purposes than just getting food into your stomach in the shortest possible time. It is a time to talk, too, and to enjoy the company of others.

What if you are in a public or a formal setting, and you don't know what is considered proper? A bit of cautious waiting and watching can cover for ignorance. You don't need to be the first to eat. However, it's still good to know a bit about manners ahead of time, because even following other people's examples is not foolproof. A man was invited to dine with a dignitary. He was eager to leave a good impression on his host. So when the host poured some hot drink onto his saucer, he did too. But when the host set the saucer on the floor for the cat, he was stumped!

Don't forget to relax and be yourself. Reserve and kindness with common sense will get you along just fine. Don't get on edge trying to do it just right. Remember, too, that the world doesn't collapse if you make some mistakes. To my knowledge, embarrassment has never been fatal to anyone!

These sample areas should help you to find a middle road in your manners. Always be sure they are the product of sincerity and not just put on for appearance's sake. This main rule is more important than all the particulars.

We'll go on now to some personal matters.

Personal Neatness

The matter of cleanliness is awkward to approach someone about, but it may be helpful here. Some time ago, this subject came up in a youth class at a Bible school. The opportunity was given for the youth to share the things they found distasteful among their friends. Of course, it was difficult to say much. So they were encouraged to put their complaints in a box by the next class time. Some of their opinions are included in the following suggestions.

Being clean means keeping the whole body clean, not just the visible part. That does not mean you should never get dirty. But there is a difference between new dirt and old dirt. You can usually tell whether someone just got dirty or whether he's been that way a long time. It's one thing to come out of the shop or barn, grimy. It's totally different to go to church that way.

Then there is odor. Should people at church be able to tell what your occupation is by the smell? Hardly. On the other hand, neither should they get the idea you work in a perfume factory! Cleanliness has a good smell all of its own—but it is a faint one. Don't be like a jet plane that leaves a vapor trail behind it.

There is also the matter of bad breath. You may have encountered it in other people. That should be incentive for you to pay some attention to your own. (If you have a problem, see if brushing your teeth or perhaps just taking a drink of water to moisten your mouth solves the problem.) Avoid breathing into others' faces as much as you can.

Hands need attention. Paying attention to nails is part of cleaning up. Granted, there may be times when hands are chapped and the dirt is so stubborn, it won't all come off. But it should be evident you gave it a good honest effort.

Your clothes have something to say about you too. Some people look as if they slept in them while others are uncomfortably fussy. Developing the habit of being neat and tidy without being vain speaks properly for Christian character. Clothes don't need to be new to be neat. In fact, they can be very old.

The way you keep your hair speaks for you. Giving it too much attention is a mark of vanity. But it is a good habit to keep your hair in place as much as is reasonably practical and possible. Also remember that the type and frequency of your haircut tells people whom you are trying to impress.

In every culture, people recognize certain trademarks as going with neatness or with sloppiness. Today, casual clothes are the popular thing. They represent the spirit of the age—loose and indifferent. This worldly spirit has encouraged young men and women to take a casual approach to Christianity. Don't be caught following the world's course. Wear the right clothes in a respectful way that lets everybody know that your allegiance is to God.

In our society, people also associate certain practices with Christians and certain other practices with the world. You owe it to them, to yourself, and to God to give a clear, clean-cut image.

Finally,

Learn to Relax

As we implied before, being too self-conscious makes it hard to act naturally. While a certain amount of self-consciousness helps to remind us to act properly, it may make us feel awkward when with others. It can make us feel clumsy and inferior. Also, being too concerned about what others are thinking of us can be a subtle form of pride. You may need to deliberately stop worrying about what others may be thinking and be satisfied to be yourself. Very likely, others do not notice your blunders or whatever you may worry about nearly as much as you think.

On the other hand, you need to avoid the pitfalls of overconfidence and arrogance. All this isn't so hard as it sounds. God can help you to be humble, confident, and comfortable, all at the same time.

The more you think about being a blessing to others and a glory to God, the more you can become free of thinking about yourself. Pay just enough attention to yourself to turn the raw material God has given you into a strong, honorable young man for Him. Then go live for Him.

Chapter 25

Peer Pressure

Did you ever come home saying, "I need new boots. My old ones are worn out. And the new kind I want is . . ."?

"Oh, I didn't know you needed new boots. What happened to yours?"

"Well, ah, er, everybody else is getting new boots this fall. I need some too. And I . . ."

Peer pressure implies being influenced by others of our own age level. It is feeling that we need what others have, or must do what they are doing. It is wanting the approval and acceptance of our age group. Few people like to be different—at least not in a way that others consider odd.

Not only young people face peer pressure. A retired man recently commented that he has to upgrade his vehicle because it does not fit in with the others' vehicles in the trailer park where he winters.

Still, youth are often more susceptible to peer pressure than other age groups. Maybe it is because they are moving beyond the home security into a larger social world. Maybe it is because they fear being rejected more than other people do. As a young man, you must find your way through these pressures, or they can be your undoing.

But peer pressure is not all bad. It can even be an asset to you. That's what much of this chapter is about. We will start on the positive side by saying that

Peer Pressure Can Be Good

God made us to influence each other. It is His way of passing values from one generation to another. Children naturally think that the way their parents do things is about right. Most farmer boys think (at least when they are young) that the kind of tractor their father has is the best.

It works the same way in spiritual and moral issues. Children pick up what their parents consider to be acceptable. When did you learn the importance of being honest? You hardly know, do you? Likely it has been an impression longer than you can remember. That is probably why young people normally accept their parents' religion, at least until they are older.

These influences are good when directed properly. If you doubt that, imagine growing up without receiving any teaching from other people! You would have to learn practically everything for yourself—the hard way. What a frustrating and painful childhood that would be!

Not only your parents, but also your grandparents, other relatives, the ministry, and teachers in the church have probably encouraged you toward doing right. While these are not necessarily your peers, they also can influence you to the good.

But coming to the matter of peer pressure, there are many ways young people can put pressure—good pressure—on each other. If one does right, it makes others feel they should too—or at least it convicts them if they don't. When other young people sing heartily in church, it makes you feel like singing too, doesn't it? Or if you look around in church and see them listening intently, it encourages you to do the same.

What others talk about affects you. If they like to talk about serious things and discuss the sermon, it helps you to want to do the same. Young people can be a real challenge to each other in ways like this. It's good to be around other young men who do that to you. One father who inspires me says that when he was young, he associated with other young men who made him "stretch a little."

But good peer pressure doesn't really make you. True, it may influence you. But you must beware of doing right only because of pressure's sake. You must decide in your own heart whether or not to embrace the true values of the Christian faith. Then these pressures can help you to be a strong young man and not just a hypocrite.

Doing right because of pressure from others will not carry you through. Sooner or later you will face tests in life when no one is with you to put pressure on you. Those tests will be of such force that only inner conviction will enable you to draw strength from God. King Joash was faithful while a faithful priest was by his side. But, sadly, when the priest had died, King Joash failed miserably.

Besides, what will you do when you face powerful peer pressures from the *wrong* direction? We must recognize that

Peer Pressure Can Be Bad

The Book of Acts describes a riot in Ephesus which shows us how peer pressure works. People rushed together and shouted for hours, and yet the Bible says that "the more part knew not wherefore they were come together." It was the popular thing to do, so they did it without even knowing what it was about.

The big question you must answer is, How will you face the pressures of your day? Are you going to be affected by the ones that are good for you or those which take you the wrong way?

In today's world, peer pressure is a powerful selling force. Advertisements give the impression that to be "in," you must buy whatever that rugged-looking young man in the ad is using. And people buy, even if it doesn't make sense and they can't afford it.

Peer pressure often comes in the form of fads. Someone starts a practice and with clever promotion gets others to fall into line. A fad can be either local or widespread. It may be a mustache in one country and long hair in another.

Fads affect clothing. One time the fad is to wear new clothes, another time to wear old clothes—or new clothes acid-treated to look old. Who knows what will be next?

If anyone knows, the clothes designers do. They change styles frequently to keep clothing sales brisk. The public meekly lays out more money to bring their wardrobes up to date. After a flood in a large city, a cleanup crew came upon a house basement packed full of dresses. Think of it—one lady, and all those dresses.

Then there are the vehicles. They have become important for far more than just transportation. Drive through town and you will see what peer pressure calls for. It may be hot rods, pickups, or whatever. Those who don't have the "right" type are doing their best to get it.

Eyeglasses used to be to look through. Now they are being made to look at. Shapes and sizes vary. The frames must be fashionable. Sometimes fashion's pendulum swings toward contacts, so people buy them.

Watches have elevated their status too. Now they are for more than just to tell time. Lately I overheard a store clerk say she had to keep her sleeve pulled down because she was wearing a cheap watch. I don't suppose she meant she was wearing a toy watch that couldn't tell the time!

Another fad I have seen gives the idea that wearing light-weight clothes when it is cold is a sign of toughness. Young men can be almost stiff with cold, but not admit it or put on a coat. Why? Pressure from others.

Peer pressure also is a major force in shaping attitudes. Usually any group develops a prevailing attitude within itself. It may be to respect their parents or to despise them. It affects whether they respect or reject the church—especially her standards or her leaders. It may be either to scorn or to respect law authorities. Powerful pressure comes on everybody to fall into line with the popular idea. The weak are pushed right into the mold.

Peer pressure can put class ratings on people. Some groups of young people, for no good reason, look down on certain people and accept others. If you belong to their group, fine. If not, you are out. Then, because of fear of being rejected, you are pressured to be partial too. This pressure amounts to deciding whom you can be friends with.

Listen to the favorite expressions certain groups use in their talk. They imitate each other. The same is true of tastes in music and recreational activities. Group pressure can even determine who is a suitable girlfriend and who is not. Courtship practices too, are molded by what others think and do. The person who lines up with wrong group pressure likely justifies himself with the idea, "Everybody is doing it."

Where you are and whom you are with naturally affects

the kind of pressure you receive. Maybe your parents have not allowed you to follow the fads. You may belong to a church that has a dress code and other restrictions to keep you from the things we talked about. Does that remove the danger of peer pressure?

No, it does not. Even within the boundaries that a faithful church draws, people somehow find room for wrong self-expression. A person can do differently from the world and still do what he does with the same spirit as the world. Granted, the way he expresses it may be subdued. His hair might be short enough, and his clothes might have the right design. But the swoops and swirls in his hair or the way he carries his clothes tells his spirit. You have probably seen that spirit at work. It is very destructive to spiritual life.

Bad peer pressure is dangerous because it often influences people more strongly than parents' desires do, or even Bible principle itself. It is especially dangerous when peer pressure urges you to do what your flesh would like to do. Then you have it coming at you from both sides—within and without.

As you can see, peer pressure can be very cruel to those who resist its force. Naturally, this helps break them down and bring them into conformity to the group.

But peer pressure doesn't need to do any of these things to you. You can be strong and overcome these tests by properly

Dealing With Peer Pressure

Who decides what effect peer pressure has on you? You know the answer to that—you decide it yourself. But do you know exactly how you decide it? It's not by shrugging off the pressure you don't want. It is by deciding whose approval you want.

Young Man, Be Strong

Looking for approval is not wrong; we all seek someone's approval. The important thing is to seek the right people's approval. By deciding what kind of people you want to accept you, you choose the direction peer pressure comes from. You must spend your time with the right people. If you deliberately expose yourself to poor influences, they will destroy your desire to do right.

You must guard your attitudes carefully. Don't let others pressure you into rejecting right and yielding to wrong. Beware of any pressure that would put you at odds with godly parents. Don't let anyone make you think you are too old to obey and honor them. The same holds true for the rules the church has made to apply Bible principles.

If you do find yourself among people who bring wrong pressure on you, resist it. Make no apologies. Beware of the pressure to be a borderline Christian. Don't compromise on anything that would make your loyalties look questionable— whether it is vehicles, hair style, clothing, or anything else.

If you want to be a strong man for the Lord, commit yourself totally to Christ and desire to have Him accept you. This will deliver you from the desire to be accepted by people who are not committed to Him.

Be more concerned about doing right than about having the approval of men. The Bible says of men who fell, "For they loved the praise of men more than the praise of God."

Finally, young man, what kind of pressure does your life put on others? Does your life encourage others to do right, or does it make it more difficult for them to do right? These are sober questions which you must answer to God. Determine not only that you will refuse wrong pressure, but that you also will do all you can to influence others in the right way.

Chapter 26

Preparing for Courtship

Most young men need no encouragement to think about this subject! That's no surprise, because it is the way God created us. Even though young men appreciate their parents' home, they begin to sense a longing for a home of their own. I had a relative who once told his father, "I'm always going to stay home with you." It was a noble expression of love, but the day came when he felt a pull even stronger than that.

Starting a home is serious business. Sometimes young men dream about it without carefully considering the responsibility involved. Granted, starting a home is one of the best things that can happen to a young man. But it can also be among the worst.

Deciding whom to marry is probably the most far-reaching move you will ever make except for the decision whether or not to be a child of God. It is a permanent, binding choice, and God meant it to be. A wife is not like a car or a house that you can change along the way.

Your wife will either help you or hurt you spiritually. I know of young men who didn't think about this when choosing their wives. They did not pay enough attention to determine spiritual interest. Later they would have liked to take life more seriously, but their wives were not interested.

Then there are future generations to consider. The course your home takes will influence the course your children's homes will take. For illustrations, look at your cousins and see how the courses your uncles and aunts took affected your cousins. The wife you choose will have a great effect on the course your home takes.

Why do I bring all this up when we are only talking about preparing for courtship? Because marriage, finally, is what courtship is all about. And underneath the pleasantness of marriage lie solemn promises.

Part of preparing for courtship is learning to

Control Your Interest

It's natural for a young man to be interested in girls. But that shouldn't be all he's interested in! If he fills his head with them, there will be little room for anything else or anyone else.

This includes God. A young man who is too interested in girls has a hard time being as involved and attentive in a worship service as he ought to be. He will find it hard to concentrate on serious Bible study and prayer.

Uncontrolled interest takes a young man into a world of fantasy and wasted time. And, the kind of girls the overinterested boys are often attracted to are not the ones who make the best wives, because those girls are often intoxicated with the same problem. So a young man who feeds this interest too much is hurting his future.

Interest in the opposite sex often begins before boys are mature enough to form proper relationships. It is not unusual for interest to develop during the later school years. Sometimes boys even think, "This is it! I have found her!"

This interest in itself is not the greater problem. As I said, a general interest is normal. The damage occurs when boys start picking specific girls and pairing up before they are old enough. This special interest often leads to teasing, being secretive, silliness, and other kinds of damaging activity.

What does a schoolboy look for in a girl, anyway? Do you think it's the things that really matter? Hardly. Or is it an attraction to an appealing face, a sparkling eye, or even pigtails?

Another difficulty with premature interest is that it stunts normal growing up. Boyhood is the time to think about many things more valuable for the time being than special friendships with girls. It's a time to learn woodworking, to go hiking, to read books, to collect stamps or butterflies, and to look forward to driving a car. It's a time to learn how to work and live unselfishly. Early interest in girls is usually selfish. It is trying to possess someone to which you have no claim.

There are other dangers. People change—especially during the growing-up years. How can a boy know what a schoolgirl will be like when she is old enough to date? He can't even know what he himself will be like. Many school-age boys and girls have shown great spiritual promise, only to prove to be bitter disappointments later.

When a young man hangs onto the idea that a certain girl is for him, it blocks his mind to other possibilities. Also, sometimes a young man and woman have an understanding for so long that they keep carrying on their relationship out of a sense of obligation rather than true love. Even if they have a happy marriage later, that early interest is not an asset to them. If anything, it robs them, because they failed to learn many other interesting things when they were younger—things that could make their marriage richer today.

What then should you do with this natural interest? In the early years, you should largely ignore it. The next step is to learn to control it. Keep it mainly to yourself. That is important, because no one outgrows the need to control his desires. Also, talk to the Lord about it, rather than discussing it with your friends. Discuss it with your parents or some spiritual adult. This way you will find it much easier to keep it as sacred as it should be.

When you control your interest, you are in a position for the Lord to lead you. You are also qualified to think about

Establishing Ideals

Even when the time for interest in women has come, you must be selective. Need I tell you that there are some types of women you must determine not to be interested in? The Book of Proverbs describes them well. Reject their offers to get friendly. Feel repulsed. Flee!

That type of woman is an extreme type, I know. Now, look at your own circles. When you take a special interest in someone, be sure you are not responding only to surface qualities. Some of the best crowd-pleasers make the poorest partners.

Some young men draw up a list of qualities they are looking for in a wife. This can help guard against the danger of being attracted to someone for flimsy, surface reasons. What should be on that list?

You already know that beauty is too near the surface to be much of an issue. But it's amazing how much young men allow that to influence them. One sharp observer remarked that the average man can see better than he can think.

Make sure you think, because a successful marriage takes much more than a beautiful wife.

What about personality? Everybody likes a nice personality. But it all depends on what's behind the personality. If character doesn't back it up, then in the tests of life, a pleasant personality has a way of vanishing.

Where does that leave us? First Peter 3:3, 4 tells us the important thing is not the outward adorning (which is all that some pretty faces and pleasant personalities are). "But let it be the hidden man of the heart, in that which is not corruptible, even the ornament of a meek and quiet spirit, which is in the sight of God of great price." The inner qualities are what count. They create a beauty that only the Christian woman has.

How can you know if someone has spiritual qualities? That is not hard. Is she giggly and lighthearted, or is she simply pleasant? Does she enjoy spiritual discussions? Does she take an interest in worship services, finding passages in her Bible or helping to sing as if her heart is in it?

There are other things to look for. Would you like to have a headstrong, unsubmissive wife? Who would? Then consider her attitude toward her parents. Does she honor and obey them? Does she enjoy submitting to the church, or does she try to slide along on the edge? Don't forget that if she shows up poorly in these matters, she will show the same attitudes in marriage—to the distress of the man who marries her.

What is her attitude toward herself? Is she often forgetting herself and thinking of others? Is she modest? Or does she dress and act so as to draw attention to herself? Put something about this on your list of ideals.

Has she learned to take responsibility? Is she quick to give a helping hand around the house? How does she treat her brothers and sisters? Does she help her little brother blow his nose? These areas may seem insignificant and unimportant now. But in real life—the home life you hope to have—they count.

The time for you to establish ideals is before you let your affection for someone start to grow. Love has a way of blinding you to the flaws another person may have. In some ways, this is fine after marriage. But don't let love decide who you think is ideal. Let your ideals decide whom you will love.

Be realistic, of course; no one is perfect. Don't be so particular that no one will satisfy you. But seek for one who is totally dedicated to God and shows His presence within.

"Who can find a virtuous woman?" Really, it's not a matter of great searching. It is more a matter of being

What You Need to Be

Sweep your own doorstep. Concentrate on being the kind of person you hope to find. Remember, the girls are observing the boys too! You and other persons with similar goals will find yourselves attracted to each other. The Lord can work out the details. Abraham's servant put it well when he went to find a wife for Isaac: "I being in the way, the Lord led me."

Let's take a look at some of the qualities in which you want to be strong.

Again we must start with spiritual qualities. Is your commitment to Jesus Christ the central point of your life? Are you having victory over sin? Are you a loyal, active church member? The list could go on. I believe you could add many spiritual qualities to the list.

Are you becoming more able to take responsibility? Marriage is a great responsibility for a young man. Are you ready (and capable) to take a woman away from her home and promise her a livelihood, love, and loyalty to her as long as you both live? Are you dependable enough to be worthy of such a trust? Have you learned financial responsibility? Have you learned to get along well enough with others to be a congenial partner in marriage? As you can see, marriage is for men, not boys.

Have you proven that you can get along with your own family? Your wife and children will be your own family too, you know. Changing homes is much like changing communities—in both cases you take yourself along. There's an old story about a man who moved into a new community. He asked his new neighbor, a wise old man, what the neighborhood was like. The old-timer asked him how it was where he came from. When the newcomer had described his old neighbors, the old-timer said, "That's the kind of neighbors you will find here too."

Thinking about courtship should challenge you to be an upright, strong individual. Does it? If not, you have not yet grasped how far-reaching courtship and marriage are. And, until you do, you cannot move ahead safely.

Finally then, what should you do when you feel God leading you to a certain person? Let's talk about

Starting a Relationship

In some countries, a young man's parents make all those decisions for him. In others, the young man does. Which is the better way?

Most young men wouldn't buy a property without asking advice. It would seem only reasonable to ask advice on a matter of far greater importance than that. Older people often understand your make-up and needs better than you do yourself. Your parents, for one example, have put much into your life up to this point, and they can help you here.

Your spiritual leaders also know things you don't know, and you ought to count them as a vital source of help. Get information and advice about the person you are interested in before you approach her.

Take your time. You should be well into your upper teens before you think seriously about approaching someone about courtship. Pray much about it. God has ways of working out what He wants. Time spent waiting for Him is well spent.

How should you go about it? You should take the initiative yourself. Don't try to get someone else to do the inquiring. A personal encounter or a letter are both proper. Let her know you would have interest in becoming better acquainted. Ask her if she would feel led to have further contact. Give her some time to consider your request. Encourage her to seek the Lord's leading also.

Some young men think such a process takes too long. They also feel they have the right to do it all by themselves. But the fact is, the more mature a person is, the less he wants to do it by himself. He realizes the importance of the matter and wants guidance and support.

Where does personal feeling come in? Certainly personal attraction and love do have an important place. But does this mean we should "fall in love"? Hardly, because people who fall in love may fall out of love just as quickly.

How should we describe true love then? True love is an intelligent attraction to someone because of her good qualities. True love develops a strong feeling, it is true, and no doubt people are right when they say, "Love is the happiest feeling in the world." But true love also develops unselfish loyalty. It helps us to sacrifice and be willing to hurt for the sake of the one we love. First Corinthians 13, the love chapter, applies to no love better than to the love between husband and wife.

When does love happen? It doesn't happen; it grows. Don't consider yourself to be deeply in love when you start dating; true love is not like that. Even if the one you are dating is a good Christian, a good cook, and a good housekeeper, you have yet to see if your interests and personality fit well with hers. But we're getting into the next chapter.

Meanwhile, young man, busy yourself with being a strong man for God, so He can lead you.

Chapter 27

Courtship

Courtship is a major step into the future. The way you go about finding a wife has a lot to do with the kind of wife you will have. Your method is somewhat like a one-way street. You want to pick that street carefully.

The question is not only, "Whom will I marry?" More important is the question, "What kind of person will I marry?" I have already been trying to help you with that question. If you have the "what kind of" settled, God can help you discover the "who." (It's not that the "who" doesn't matter, but I don't know your personal preferences and cannot help you with that.)

Courtship has its difficult aspects. You must make decisions about the future when you don't know the future. You face uncertainties that only God can be certain about. Your girlfriend might even say, "I'd rather not," when you thought surely God was leading you to continue your friendship. Just getting started in courtship may be hard for you if you sense the magnitude of it all.

What is the answer to these difficult questions? Going back to God is always the answer, even though you do not always understand Him. If you let Him lead you during this time, courtship can be a wonderful part of your life. It can prepare you for a rewarding marriage and leave you a stronger person.

Not every man ends up the better for his courtship. The girl he dates or the things he does while dating can damage him spiritually or even destroy him. This does not need to happen to you.

We won't spend much time talking about the type of person to choose in this chapter because we discussed it in the previous one. I want to remind you again, though, that you must be sure that you are looking for the right kind of person in the right kind of places. It is the only way to be able to discover God's purpose for you.

Now let's focus our attention on how you should build your friendship with the person you believe God has led you to. If you want God to bless you, you must honor His

Guiding Principles

The first of these guiding principles is simply this: courtship is serious. Certainly, God wants you to enjoy it. But He never intended it to be a frivolous pastime. He wants it to be a happy search for His will in the matter of finding a life companion.

This means that courtship is not for everyone. Or it could mean that courtship will not take place until ten years down the road. Sometimes God has special plans for someone, which do not include marriage. For such a person, staying single is noble. Single people in God's will have a calling that is as meaningful and rewarding as any married person has. In fact, some such people have been particularly useful to God. The apostle Paul is a good example of this. So is Christ Himself.

But we will assume for the moment that God has led you into courtship. A major purpose of courtship is to discover if the person you feel attracted to is really for you. You have admired her from a distance and are pleased with what you see. You may also have gotten advice that encouraged you to become better acquainted. But there are still some things you need to learn about each other.

Courtship is a time to explore the spiritual side of each other. (The woman needs to be just as concerned about you as you are about her.) You should share and compare convictions. Your goals for the Christian life must be very similar. Your friend must show a love for Christ that is all her own. She should not just take a "yes, I think so too" attitude.

Discussing spiritual things will raise some practical questions. You both will need to agree on what church to be loyal to. I know of a young man who was interested in a girl who was a member of a church that was not totally Scriptural. He wisely waited until that person became part of a Scriptural church before he tried to start a special friendship. There have been others, though, who couldn't wait. They have found themselves drawn into a poor church setting because they compromised Bible principle for the sake of a friendship. That is one good reason to choose a companion from your own faith and practice.

Courtship is also a time for closer character study. Both of you need to know how the other faces life and solves problems. Can your friend apply Bible principles to those problems? Does she show the stable Christian character traits that will stand the test of time? This reveals spirituality.

Then comes the social compatibility test. What do you

enjoy? Do you both like books? What about gardening? Do you both like to sit and talk? Can you communicate to each other how you "really" feel?

How this compatibility works is a mystery. Sometimes the temperamental make-up of the couple is very similar, and the relationship blossoms. Other couples' temperaments are vastly different and yet blend very well. All we can say is, God brings both kinds of pairs together. It's the genius of love at work!

You will need to agree on secular issues as well. The area you will live in and the kind of work you will do need to be agreeable to both. Normally, when you agree on nearly everything else, these questions do not create a problem. But you must be determined to keep them from creating one. If either of you has misgivings about what the other person expects, you will need to settle it before the relationship can grow comfortably.

Some couples brush questions like these aside. They are sure their love can resolve any such issues. But personal preferences don't go away on the wedding day and can become a source of tension. Remember that Satan will use anything to destroy harmony. Many times he has used things that seemed at one time to be too small to pay attention to.

Courtship is the time to establish good communication. Without it, even a marriage is only a surface relationship. Communication means being able to share your opinions and feelings honestly without fearing rejection. You need to feel that your friend understands you, or at least sympathizes with you. You should feel more and more comfortable with her as time goes on. That does not mean there will never be difficulties or misunderstandings. It does mean, though, that you are able to work through them satisfactorily.

Young Man, Be Strong

Another great guiding principle in courtship is this: keep yourself pure. Happy as your friends may be about your friendship, someone does not like it, and he is the devil. Never forget that you and your girlfriend have a busy enemy. Satan tries hard to spoil what God intends to be holy and happy.

Regarding purity, the first question most people think of is, "Just how much physical contact is proper during courtship?" Some people say that physical contact actually helps a courtship. They say it is a way of expressing love that cannot be done any other way. They scoff at those who question the temptations that come along with physical contact. They say that if it doesn't go too far, there is nothing wrong with it.

But what, after all, is purity? Is it only in keeping from certain acts that are "going too far"? Or can impurity take place without any act at all? Matthew 5:28 can help us: "But I say unto you, That whosoever looketh on a woman to lust after her hath committed adultery with her already in his heart." This shows us that we are dealing with far more than actions—we must answer for our thoughts.

This verse applied to courtship means, "Don't do anything that would tempt you to think lustful thoughts." Any man should understand what that means. For example, shaking hands with a woman normally does not arouse impure feelings. Holding hands on the sofa normally does. As long as you and your friend are not married, you need to be careful not to do anything that would bring you under condemnation from this verse. Physical contact does not help a dating couple become better acquainted. In fact, it smothers communication of the spirit and soul. It crowds out concern for holiness and right. It shifts the focus from the spiritual to the physical. And when physical stimulation ignites, it clouds better judgment and demands more freedom. And that can only end in frustration and regret.

Physical contact is not the right way to express love outside of marriage. Anyone with true love wants to protect his companion's purity. When a young man and woman agree to protect each other without even having to mention it, they are on solid ground for a rewarding courtship.

Young man, you want to come to the marriage altar with full assurance that God is pleased with your courtship, don't you? Now is the time to establish your guidelines. Accept the counsel of others; you don't need to learn the hard way. Enough other people have already done that. Remember that Satan starts with little things, and determine that you will avoid the temptations of handholding, hugging, kissing, and suchlike during courtship. You will never be sorry for being reserved.

There are various ways that inroads can start. Be careful to avoid suggestive responses and talk. Subjects that are of a private nature should also be closely guarded. Drawing hearts on letters and setting pictures of each other around too freely can produce difficulty. Don't feel obligated to always be talking about her.

Purity makes the wedding day all the more meaningful. Any liberties that couples have taken before marriage now show up to be liabilities rather than assets. Enough people have said they are glad they were pure during courtship, and enough other people have said they are sorry they weren't, to prove that God's way is best.

These guidelines were not given because I distrust you. I don't question your motives or your friend's. But I know human nature. James 5:17 tells us that even Elijah "was a man subject to like passions as we are." None of us is exempt from temptation. That is why a "no touch" courtship is the only safe and the most rewarding way. You should have a clear understanding about this with your friend from the start.

Without question, guidelines are good. But let me caution you; no amount of rules will automatically guard you against failure. You personally must have the conviction to do right; then guidelines can help you.

These are guiding principles. Now we will discuss

Practical Suggestions

You should be accountable to someone for all the time you and your girlfriend spend together. It is for your protection. Accept direction, and don't forget to exercise some self-discipline of your own.

To keep proper reserve, you and your girlfriend need to limit the amount of time you spend together on a date. Being together alone too long introduces difficulty. If you travel long distances, do it with others. For the same reason, you need to guard the frequency of the times you spend together. Did you know that it takes more maturity for a couple to limit their dates than it does to be together too much?

What you do when you are together is very important because it will affect your values and appetites. A couple that attends a church service is in a much better position to keep pure than the couple that stays home by themselves. Why? Because couples that isolate themselves in their own little world have more temptations than those who share with others.

Plan for your dating to surround spiritual activities. Naturally, you should support your local church services. Dating gives no exemptions from your duties (privileges) as a member. Services provide an excellent basis for a real spiritual relationship with your friend. Discussing the message together will help you to grow spiritually and understand each other better.

The church usually provides other activities too that can benefit you. Do the young people get together and sing sometimes? Or do they give out Christian literature? Those are just a few examples. Don't miss the "giving and the getting" that Christian service activities provide.

Visiting is another good way to enjoy each other's company. Getting to know each other's families is important. Your girlfriend will want to meet your family, and they will want to meet her. You also will want to get to know her family. When a person marries, he often gets more of the rest of the family than he expected! Also don't neglect visiting the aged and sick people who need encouragement.

It is all right to do some things for personal enjoyment if it does not interfere with spiritual life. Going for a walk, looking at photo albums, reading a book, painting, or things like that can be a way of getting to know each other better. What about playing games like Parcheesi? Well, games are not wrong in themselves, but they are not so uplifting as some of the other activities we mentioned. Conversation over a game board will probably not have as good a quality as conversation over a photo album. I recommend leaving the games mostly for the children.

You should spend part of your time on each date worshiping God together. Bible study and prayer should be part of your dating activities. Discuss your personal devotional lives together. Study and discuss a book on Bible doctrine or something similar. This will give you a solid foundation on which to build your relationship. You will grow spiritually as you do this together. And it will prepare you to have family devotions after marriage.

Young Man, Be Strong

Young man, it's your duty to set the pace in courtship. The man is to be the head of the home. So it is his responsibility to lead out in courtship activities. The woman you are interested in has a right to know what kind of leader you are.

Then there are activities you should encourage each other in. Discuss books you have read. Or both read the same book separately and discuss it together. Write some letters in each other's absence. You can learn a lot about each other by doing this.

Remember that dating is not everything. Stay involved in your own family's activities. Don't let your courtship swallow up all your thinking time. Live a normal life, with courtship as one of the special parts of it. It's a sign of maturity to incorporate courtship into a full life in which you live for the Lord in many ways, not just one.

How can you know if your courtship interests and activities are on the right track? Several simple tests can help you. First, does your courtship make you want to be a better, stronger Christian? Second, do you feel comfortable that all you are doing is pleasing to God? Third, is your courtship such that it will contribute to a strong Christian home in the future? If so, young man, you are in a very honorable position. Don't lose it.

If you are not dating, file these ideas away and determine to live by them if that time comes. Be a strong young man for God, now. Then you can enjoy the present and also be prepared for whatever God has for you in the future.

Chapter 28

What Christian Service Is for You

I have a proposal to make to you. But first, let me tell you an old story from the days of slavery and make some observations.

A strong young slave was put on the auction block. He looked able to do an enormous amount of work, so the bidding was lively. But the young man was bitter. Why should he be treated like an animal? He already hated the man who would buy him.

The bidding stopped. The buyer stepped forward. He saw the seething hatred in the young man's eyes, but he was not discouraged. He took his new possession aside. Looking him in the eye, he said, "I have bought you. You are mine. I bought you . . . to set you free."

When it all dawned on the slave, he threw himself at the buyer's feet. "Master," he said, "I'll serve you forever." No longer was he a resentful slave, but a willing servant.

Was the slave's response overdone? Hardly. What else could he do when he really grasped what he had been saved from? And who else would he rather be close to the rest of his life than such a kind redeemer?

God too, buys—or rather, buys back—people who are in slavery to sin and the old nature. But then He goes far beyond just buying us and setting us free. He makes us sons! Think of it! Not only "a servant, but a son . . . an heir of God through Christ," as Galatians 4:7 says. How can we help but cast ourselves at His feet and say with our slave friend, "Master, I'll serve You forever!"

Some young men say they are glad to be sons of God. They want the position and the benefits. But when it comes to the "serving forever" part, no thanks. They forget that if a Christian does not accept a servant's place, he will not be much of a son. In fact, he will not be a son at all.

Sons of God are partners with God. His work is their work. Second Corinthians 6:1 says, "We then, as workers together with him [God] . . ." The closer the relationship between Father and sons, the greater the cooperation.

God the Father and Jesus are the greatest example of cooperation. Jesus said in John 9:4, "I must work the works of him that sent me." He even said, "My meat [my food] is to do the will of him that sent me, and to finish his work." His whole life centered around this one aim. "I come to do thy will, O God," was His banner. You too must always be asking, "What does God want from me?"

To answer this question, ask yourself another: How did God treat Jesus, His only begotten Son? Did God let Jesus off easily because of who He was? Did God spare Jesus from anything difficult? Of course not! What more difficult and demanding work could have been given to anyone than was given to Jesus? Christ's life was not easy. He is God's greatest proof that

Service Means Suffering

In fact, the Bible promises as much. "For even hereunto were ye called: because Christ also suffered for us, leaving us an example, that ye should follow his steps" (1 Peter 2:21). "Yea, and all that will live godly in Christ Jesus shall suffer persecution" (2 Timothy 3:12).

This suffering may not always come in the form of physical violence. It may come when people scoff at you for the way you dress or the things you do or do not do. It may mean being looked at as odd or even a little naïve. Even if it comes from those who profess to believe as you do, don't let that turn you aside from the narrow way to heaven.

Those who are not willing to suffer often turn back in the day of difficulty. The *Martyrs Mirror* tells not only of many who triumphantly faced death, but also of those who recanted rather than suffer. Peter warns us, "Forasmuch then as Christ hath suffered for us in the flesh, arm yourselves likewise with the same mind" (1 Peter 4:1). In other words, *forewarned* is "fore-armed." Expect to suffer, and you will be the stronger when you need to suffer.

The apostle Paul gives us another vivid picture of Christian service. "Thou therefore endure hardness, as a good soldier of Jesus Christ." A soldier expects to suffer. He foregoes all the normal comforts and interests for a greater cause. He is ready even to lay his life on the line to help that cause. Suffering and death do not frighten him. They only make him braver. Seeing yourself as a soldier of Jesus Christ makes suffering easier to bear.

Another thing you must understand about serving the Lord is that

Service Means Sacrifice

Some people want to serve God with what is left over. If they have any time left over, they will help their needy neighbor. If they have any money left over, they will put a bit of it into the offering. If they have enough energy left over, they will help in distributing Christian literature. If it doesn't interfere with their own projects, they will do something for Him. If . . . If . . . If . . . Without deliberate carefulness, we can become like that ourselves.

Let's face it. Serving God takes sacrifice. Usually, something that doesn't cost much isn't worth much.

The important thing is not so much what you actually get done—it's your attitude that counts. Once you begin sacrificing for the Lord, God will accept your service. Jesus complimented the widow who gave two mites, saying she gave more than all the rest. Was it the amount she gave? No. It was that she had sacrificed more than anyone else.

What about time? Have you begun to sacrifice it for the Lord? Sure, you need to work, eat, and sleep. But what about your extra time? Do you look for things to do that are a help to others? Can you give up your projects or plans for the sake of others? Can you be glad about it? Or do you feel that others ought to notice and appreciate what you are doing, or else it isn't worth doing?

This matter of sacrificing time brings me to my proposal for you. You realize that many young people give a year or two—some less, some much more—in what we call voluntary service. During the years of the draft, our nonresistant young men were given the privilege to take some form of alternate service. Many others have served the church for a period of time on various mission fields. Incidentally, you don't need to go a long distance from home to find a mission field.

My proposal to you is that you consider giving a block of your life to this type of service. There are a number of good reasons for this.

First, it is a way of putting God first. It shows that you are willing to postpone your own interests for His kingdom.

Next, it is one of the ways that the Lord's work gets done. Look at any effective part of His work, and you will see those who are sacrificing for it.

For another thing, giving time for a term of service usually produces spiritual growth.

Finally, regardless of what way you serve the Lord afterwards, your experience in voluntary service is valuable because of the way it enlarges your horizons.

Consider it at least. We realize that some young men can serve the Lord better by sticking close to home than they could anywhere else. But let that be your reason for staying home, if you stay, rather than saying, "I just didn't think of voluntary service."

You might ask what you can do. Ask God. Ask your church. Keep your ears and eyes open. Start by doing what is at hand. Don't idly wait for some great opportunity, because if you do, you will miss it when it comes. Doing little things open doors to greater opportunities. Remember, it is the little things that seem to impress God the most.

Whether or not you do something "special" for a year or two, make sacrificial service a way of life for you. If you see something to be done and you have the power to do it, there should not be any question but that you will do what you can.

Don't waste your life on yourself. See service not only as a duty, but as a privilege. It is a way of expressing your love to God for what He has done for you.

Chapter 29

Being a Soul Winner

How would you feel if you suddenly heard that you inherited a million dollars? Could you keep quiet about it? It would be hard, wouldn't it? That's probably not a fair question, because neither of us expects to inherit a million dollars. But I want you to think how hard it is to keep quiet when you are glad about something.

Years ago some men were excited about their religion. The authorities called them in, threatened them, and told them to be quiet about it. But the apostles answered, "We cannot but speak the things which we have seen and heard" (Acts 4:20).

Knowing the Lord and being one of His children is a wonderful privilege. But it is also a responsibility, because He calls us to share the good news of what has happened to us.

The work of winning souls must be part of us, never too far in the back of our minds. Opportunities come and go so quickly. If we aren't ready, we will miss them. I have a painful memory of this happening to me when I was a young man.

I had stopped at a business place to take care of an errand

for a friend. Two clerks were at the counter. After discussing my errand with me, one of them left for a moment. The other, who was standing by, suddenly said, "How come you don't swear or smoke?"

I was taken aback. I had been in a hurry, and thoughts like these had been too far from my mind. I sputtered—I tried to think of what to say. But before I got much of anything said, my clerk came back, other customers came, and the man with the question was gone. How painful! Have you ever had that happen to you? And I can't pretend that this was the only time I didn't get everything said I should have.

So, young man, we are in this together. We want to be as effective as we can for the Lord in this great work, don't we? You know it takes courage. And it may seem a bit uncomfortable at first. But, like so many other things, the more we do of it, the easier it becomes.

But it takes more than just knowing what to say. We must start with ourselves as individuals. We need to understand

What It Takes to Be a Soul Winner

Remember, young man, it is very difficult to share something you don't have—or that isn't real to you. If you would witness effectively, it has to be in your system. Otherwise, you will be like the person who said he felt "like a half-full cup trying to run over!" People are touched only when they realize that what you are telling them you have experienced yourself.

As you can see, witnessing is not only telling others what God wants to do for them; it is telling them what He has done for you. When you expose your own past need and your present peace, you can assure them that there is hope for them.

Not only must you be genuine when other people look

at you; you must take the right attitude when you look at them. Some people seem to look at witnessing as if they were parcel post delivery men. *Rap. Rap.* "A package for you, sir. Will you please sign here? Thank you and good day."

But witnessing is much more than just delivering a message of judgment to come or of the love of God and then going away thinking, "Now that's done. I told him." Witnessing means caring for people. It means feeling their need and being saddened by their condition. The high priest in the Old Testament illustrates this. He wore an ephod with the names of the twelve tribes of Israel written on it. He was to keep the people close to his heart.

We must learn to care. But how? Part of the secret is to take a deep interest in people in ordinary ways. Find out what their names are at least. Say, "How are you today?" and truly hear them when they answer. If they are the kind who like to talk, take time to listen. If they are the quiet type, don't just ask questions. Do some of the talking to let them get to know you too.

Part of caring is to be touched by their physical needs if they have any. Many times this is the foremost concern in the needy person's mind. If he feels that you don't really care about his health and physical welfare, he will doubt that you are really concerned for him spiritually.

If we are not sensitive to others, we can get wrapped up in our own little world. We can think of our plans and projects and forget to look for opportunities to do something meaningful for others. Give your neighbor a hand when you can. A good deed out of a good heart can be worth a thousand words of admonition, because it proves your message.

The most important way to care is to think about the tragedy of a lost soul. It is a great loss in two ways. First, it is total loss to the person who will be eternally separated from God. Also, it is a loss to God. Christ came and died to save them as much as any of the rest of us. If they are lost, God is robbed of a soul He longed to have with Him in glory.

Not only must we see people as God sees them; we must see our own special opportunities. Young men have an opportunity to witness that we older ones don't. Many people understand why men my age start looking down the road more seriously. But they don't expect that from young men. They know too many young men who don't stand for anything. So they take notice when a young man clearly identifies himself as one of God's people. In fact, they may even seek you out to find out what it's really about.

What an opportunity! And what a responsibility. I was told of an unsaved young man who sought out a group of Christian young people. He was so disappointed in what he found when he got to know them better that he gave up his search. How sad. But it shows that people want to know if your religion is for real—inside and out.

Recently a stranger approached one of our young brethren in the Seattle airport. The stranger wanted to know what religion the young man represented. Then he asked more questions. And he did not want to know what the young man's church or his parents believed—he wanted to know what the young man himself believed! The world is waiting to know whether you are for real or whether you are just parroting what someone else believes.

We had some neighbors who were quite open to discuss spiritual matters. One day the man turned to my wife and said he wanted to ask her some questions. He wanted to know whether she really believed in what she was doing or if it was forced on her. This, too, illustrates what I have been saying.

There are no cut-and-dried ways to witness, but here are a few suggestions on

How to Handle Opportunities

This part of the chapter will not be a complete list of do's and don'ts. We will discuss ideas on how to work with various situations, but no two situations will be exactly alike. You have to take them as they come and let the Lord work through you at the moment without planning ahead of time how it will all work out.

First, you need confidence. Did you ever feel you wanted to witness for the Lord, but just didn't know how to say it? Or the time was right, but nothing came? Don't despair! A certain amount of awkwardness is normal for a young Christian. Not knowing what to say can lead you to depend more fully on the Lord.

A man who is never at a loss for words might yet need to learn that his own words aren't what God can use. You can outtalk a person without winning him, and you can win him without outtalking him. So don't feel as if what you said was useless because it did not seem to be as persuasive as you had hoped.

Another reason for feeling awkward may be that you haven't expressed yourself enough to feel comfortable. A good way to learn to express yourself is to discuss spiritual things with your family and friends. Ask questions and share what you believe. Be active in your Sunday school class. Listening to older people and sharing with them will help you to express yourself more freely.

Granted, a young man who is shy and quiet no matter

what the subject is should not feel guilty if he is a bit slow
of tongue when talking about spiritual things. But if the
"life of the party" type of person suddenly has nothing to
say when the conversation turns to a spiritual subject, something is wrong. Regardless of whether you are quiet or outgoing, you ought to be, as Peter said, "ready always to give
an answer to every man that asketh you a reason of the
hope that is in you."

As was suggested before, it is important for you to relate
to unsaved people as a friend—not as their judge. Show your
interest in them in a general way. Let them tell you about
the worthwhile things that interest them. Ask questions
that can lead to serious matters. Asking about their family,
their occupation, and their future plans can open doors.

A man asked a young man about his life's plan. The young
man said he planned to get an education.

"Then what?"

"Get a good job and make lots of money."

"Then what?"

"Well, finally I'll retire."

"Then what?"

"Oh, ah, I don't know."

The stage was set, and the man led the young man to
think seriously about salvation.

When you ask about their spiritual condition, let them
tell you about it rather than letting them feel that you are
accusing them. Many people will say things about themselves that they would resent if someone else said it.

Sometimes it is hard to know how much pressure to put
on. Too much pressure can repulse people. But if we are too
easygoing, they may wonder how urgent our concern is. I
have missed it both ways. One man said I came on too strong.

Another said that if he believed what I said I believed, he would be far more radical than I. Maybe they were just making excuses, but it does show that we must have wisdom from God while working with the lost. We cannot force them. We must try to lead them to the Lord.

Were you ever afraid of being asked questions you couldn't answer while witnessing? Many people are. But after all, must we have all the answers before we try? No. Of course, we want to answer all the questions we can. But I suspect that people are more interested in how we react than in what we say. If you know the answer, give it humbly. If you don't know the answer, say so. Avoid being argumentative.

The most powerful witness is a simple testimony of what God has done for you. An avowed atheist I met while traveling resisted and reasoned away the tangible evidences of the existence of God. But when I told him how that in my heart I know God exists because of my personal relationship with Him, he began to think more seriously and not so argumentatively.

In the courtroom, nobody speaks more powerfully than an eyewitness. People are looking for the man who can say, "It happened to me!" even if he stumbles over his words. Do not miss the opportunity to tell it. Then be sure to tell them that what happened to you can happen to them too. Recommend it to them.

Don't try to have the last word. Let God have it. Give what He has given you, and let His Spirit use that. Try to avoid tensions, because people will likely remember feelings of tension more than the Gospel you are trying to share.

The only way to be prepared is to stay in touch with God. You must be sure that salvation is real to you—and very close to the surface. Then you can depend on God to help you testify and work in the other person's heart.

So far we talked mainly about using opportunities. Last, we need to discuss a few ways of

Making Opportunities

Not everybody gives us an opportunity to share the Gospel. Don't we have any responsibility to them? The answer to that is clear: yes. How can we best do it?

Give God a chance to make opportunities. Pray about it. Have you ever asked God to open the door? Try it. It works. Just be ready to go through the door when He opens it.

Literature provides a good way of leaving the Gospel with people. A young man in the Seattle airport who was questioned by a stranger didn't have much time to talk. But he left some literature with the man. Several weeks later, he got a letter from him. It's good to have your name on the literature you give, so that you can be of further assistance.

Inviting and encouraging people to attend your church is a way of opening doors. Naturally, it is important to have a Scriptural fellowship to recommend them to. Then when they do come, take them in warmly and help them to feel welcome.

Pray for the missionaries your church supports, and add your money to the offering for them. Read papers that tell what they are doing, and pray about what you read. Don't be like the story told about some fishermen. They spent lots of time discussing and debating the best ways to catch fish. They had seminars and meetings to perfect it to a fine art. But there was one problem—they never got around to actually fishing!

That can happen in soul winning too. Even though we may not be able to do it as well as we would like, we must work at it. It's like one active soul winner said to a critic, "I like my way of doing it better than your way of not doing it."

Young man, be up and doing. God wants the Gospel to be living in you. Then He wants you to live the Gospel. Then He can use you to spread the Good News. And you will be the stronger for it.

Chapter 30

Young Man, Be Strong

Elisha served his master, Elijah, faithfully. He was known as the man who poured water on the hands of Elijah. He followed Elijah from city to city through rivers and valleys and over the mountains. They traveled through thick and thin together.

But the day came when suddenly Elijah was gone. Only his mantle lay at Elisha's feet. Elisha was left alone. Now it was his day. What was he going to do?

In your mind's eye, see him slowly stoop and pick up the mantle. He starts back toward the river they had last crossed together. At the bank he stops, hesitates, and then cries, "Where is the Lord God of Elijah?" (Is He with me as He was with my Master? Does He accept me for His servant?) With the mantle he smites the waters of Jordan.

Elisha was not long in finding out where Elijah's God was. The waters parted, and he passed over. Full of assurance that God was with him, he began a life of faithful service to God.

That, young man, is my prayer for you—that you discover and have this God for your very own. My prayer is that God has been able to speak to you through this book—that you would feel Him calling you to a life of noble faithfulness—and that you would call on Him in return from the depths of your heart as Elisha did.

God is still looking for those who will serve Him. He wants you to serve this generation in all honesty and sincerity. He wants you to be among those who pass on the truth from your generation to the next. Can He count on you?

If you would be strong, you must flee all that threatens to defeat and destroy you. Crucify the lures of the world, the temptations, and the lusts of your own sinful nature. You cannot do it by yourself. You can do it only by trusting in God and living within His will for you.

If you would be strong, you must take advantage of all the resources God has made available to you. You must walk in His Spirit, live by His Word, and relate properly to His church. You must honor those who are over you and live in constant submission to Jesus Christ. You must live in purity and a good conscience.

"My son, be strong in the grace that is in Christ Jesus" is the best counsel anyone could give. With the grace of God as your strength, you can succeed. You can be useful and pleasing to God. You can indeed be an "example of the believers."

Remember, son, that this life is not the end. It is but a short space of time in your endless existence. Therefore, live for eternity now. Set your goal on heaven. Determine that you will not let anything endanger your safe arrival there. Heaven will be worth it all.

And now, young man, farewell. Be strong and of a good courage.